the
view
from
rock
bottom

STEPHANIE TAIT

HARVEST HOUSE PUBLISHERS
EUGENE, OREGON

Cover design by Kara Klontz Design

Cover photos © oley / Shutterstock

The View from Rock Bottom

Copyright © 2019 by Stephanie Tait
Published by Harvest House Publishers
Eugene, Oregon 97408
www.harvesthousepublishers.com

ISBN 978-0-7369-7222-2 (pbk.)
ISBN 978-0-7369-7223-9 (eBook)

Library of Congress Cataloging-in-Publication Data is on file at the Library of Congress, Washington, DC.

Printed in the United States of America

19 20 21 22 23 24 25 26 27 / BP-RD / 10 9 8 7 6 5 4 3 2 1

For Brent

I can scarcely imagine the glory of the table before you now,
but I suspect you're still saving a seat beside you for Aidan.

Contents

Foreword

Nichole Nordeman

Years ago I read a book called *The Gift of Pain*, cowritten by renowned surgeon Dr. Paul Brand and Philip Yancey. Dr. Brand had spent a good deal of his distinguished medical career studying, understanding, and treating people with leprosy. Among endless misconceptions about leprosy, there is a common belief that the disease's victims succumb to death from the diseased flesh itself. In truth, most deaths from leprosy result from painlessness-related injury or damage. Nerve damage has removed the ability for a person to feel pain, and therefore there is no intuitive ability to avoid or withdraw from it. If you can't experience the agony of your broken foot, there is nothing to prevent you from running on it, nor would you know to pull your hand back from an open flame.

Brand's integral study on the effects of the absence of physical pain translates easily to our spiritual and emotional lives. Pain is a gift. It instructs. It warns. Its tutelage is harrowing. Agonizing. And yet it shapes our very sacred souls.

One of those dear suffering-shaped souls has written the special book you're holding right now. I became familiar with Stephanie Tait the way many people find themselves in unexpected friendship these days…online. Over time, she has shared pieces of her story on social media and was gracious in telling me how songs I'd written had met her in some very dark places. Wisely, someone persuaded her to take us into the deeper parts of her story on these pages.

Stephanie joins a large club of those of us who were church-going, Bible-believing, good-choice-making, clean-living Christian kids. We did all these things. And then we were ready for all the blessings. Ready for the fulfilled promises. Did our part the way we were told to and were ready for God to make good on His end. Ready and still waiting. More waiting. And not at all ready for year after year of loss. Grief. Financial ruin. Physical devastation. Darkness. And despair.

The book you are holding is one woman's arduous and bravely personal examination of how wrong our theology is about suffering. How damaged our lens is. In story after story of her own broken journey, she shakes off the idea that our lives are meant to be merely survived with God's help, and she gently invites us to see the gift in our pain. What it points us to. What it leads us away from. How it gathers us uniquely into the arms of our community, our confidants, and our Savior. Digging into sacred Scripture, not as anecdotal hopey verses, but as the kind of crinkled-up and stained road map you dig out of your pocket to pore over when you can't make sense of yourself or the world around you.

Thank you, Stephanie, for the wildly vulnerable decision to allow us to bear witness to your journey and your relationship with pain. Thank you for respecting suffering for the teacher it is, and for respecting us as the students we will all be, at one time, whether or not we're ready. Because no one ever is.

Preface

If you picked up this book to hear a testimony of how God worked even the seemingly terrible parts of a life into a beautiful surprise ending where with a little hindsight everything suddenly made sense...

If you're walking through pain and have reached out in your desperation to this book, hoping to hear a story of someone who's already made it successfully to the other side...

If you're waiting for your prayer to be answered and are looking to my story to assure yourself that God will one day give you the desires of your heart if you only hold on a little longer...

If you're weary and broken and longing for someone to show how to get past this season of struggle or how to identify the lesson God is surely trying to teach you in all this so He will finally allow you to move beyond it...

I'm sorry, dear friend, but *this* is not that book.

When I set out to write, I knew I was walking into something that would challenge me beyond anything I had ever experienced. Much like the old adage that reminds us what happens when we pray for patience, when you commit to exploring the depths of God's presence in suffering you have to be fully prepared for Him to faithfully provide the source material you need. He has walked me through more pain than I ever thought possible to bear, and if I had known the details of His plan from the start, I likely would have pleaded for Him to pass me over for this calling.

This, my friend, is a present-tense testimony. This book springs directly from a heart still raw with grief and a body still inflicted with very real pain and disease. I have written this book not as a memoir of a journey I once had, but as letters from a woman still very much traveling this same road with God. A woman who's still not sure exactly how His plans will unfold. As one of my former pastors would commonly say, "None of us has arrived yet, least of all me."

I can't give you a story with a happy ending, because my story doesn't have an ending yet.

There will be no page where I come to the beautiful realization that my seven miscarriages were perfectly timed blessings that led me to adopt seven orphans from Africa into our home and hearts.

There will be no page where I share that God miraculously cured my Lyme disease to show His glory and power, and I've now gone on to live in health and prosperity, writing and speaking about my experiences.

There will be no page where I can tie a bow on top of my testimony and share in an articulate past-tense narrative all the specific reasons for the suffering God walked my family through, and how His plan became perfectly clear to me once I was safely on the other side.

A friend of mine reached out to me when I began this project and asked, "Why write the book now? Why not wait until you're better so you can write the whole story, ending and all?"

Because my message is ultimately this: It's not about the ending. It's not about when healing comes, or if it ever comes at all. It's not about proving God's faithfulness by showing exactly how He provided for me. It's not about helping people hold on through the hard times by promising that it's all going to work out in a way they can see and understand later.

No, this book is about destroying all of those ideas and expectations and replacing them with something so much harder but ultimately so much more fulfilling. It's a book about finding the good *in* suffering, even if the healing never comes. It's a book about seeing the faithfulness of a good and loving God, even in the valley of the shadow of death. This was never meant to be a book about holding on through the hard seasons, but rather about finding the joy and growth and holy intimacy of a God who has met me within them.

From within my pain I've made the choice to lean even deeper into His Word, to share what He is teaching me, and to continue to preach these truths to my own heart just as much as to yours. I won't pretend to have all the answers, but I will promise you this: I can confidently testify that God has been unswervingly faithful, and His mercies are new every morning (Lamentations 3:22-23). I can tell you that He has revealed Himself more to me in my deepest pain than in any other experience I've had on earth. I can tell you that I have learned more about true joy from my suffering than from any earthly happiness. I can tell you that I fervently believe that buried inside my Lyme disease is a 15-year love letter, one sent from a God passionately pursuing me and drawing me into a deeper intimacy with Him than I ever knew was possible on this side of eternity.

Just as my pain carried His love letter to me, this book now serves as the letter I penned back in response—to express my gratitude for His faithfulness, to explore the depths of this new intimacy I've found in our relationship, and to try to somehow articulate this love in a way that may draw you, dear reader, into experiencing a deeper relationship with Him as well. My prayer for you is that the truths He has shown me will spill off these pages and come alive in you, helping you discover His perfect peace in the midst of your own storms, unmitigated joy in the face of heartache, and both passion and purpose springing from the places you experience your deepest pain.

This work will not be easy, but it will be purposeful. We can confidently walk forward to explore the valley of the shadow of death because we hold firmly to the promises of the One who has already gone before us and claimed our final victory. "In me," said Jesus, "you may have peace. In the world you will have tribulation. But take heart; I have overcome the world" (John 16:33).

Chapter 1

Great Expectations

There is something in us, as storytellers and as listeners to
stories, that demands the redemptive act, that demands that
what falls at least be offered the chance to be restored.

Flannery O'Connor[1]

This book began on a bathroom floor, a seed unknowingly planted as I lay on the cold linoleum and watered with the very real tears of unspeakable brokenness and grief. It's only in hindsight I'm able to see the years of cultivation that brought me to a place where my broken heart and empty hands were ready to receive. I'll try to rewind a little, to somehow explain the events that brought me to that floor.

That summer, my family had traveled to Oregon to visit relatives when we began to feel unexpected nudges from the Holy Spirit. These started out small, prompting a few—very hypothetical— conversations in which my husband, Bobby, and I mused on what it might be like to live in a place like Oregon. We were both growing increasingly disillusioned with life back in the San Francisco Bay Area, with a local culture dominated by never-ending busyness and a cost of living that was exorbitantly disproportionate compared to just about anywhere else in the United States. We knew that living there was taking a heavy toll on us. Bobby loved his career in computer software development, but it is a field in which unexpected layoffs and even overnight closures of entire companies are routine. Every few years it seemed we endured the stress of another surprise job loss, and each time my husband had to face the competitive Silicon Valley job market as a slightly older candidate, in a profession where age and seniority are more liability than asset. It was a cycle we didn't see ending anytime soon. Plus, with the median price of a family home rapidly approaching a million dollars at the time (yes, you read that correctly), even my husband's respectable salary as a programmer was simply not enough to reliably support the basic costs of living.

It wasn't for lack of trying. Early in our marriage we had earnestly set out to make the numbers work by buying a foreclosed town house in a low-income neighborhood. That was in 2008, when the housing market had just taken its historic crash, leaving the real-estate listings littered with underpriced foreclosures, providing a once-in-a-lifetime opportunity for us to be able to purchase a home in the area. Even though the town house was located in a struggling and economically depressed neighborhood, it was still a relatively safe one, and we had hoped that by living somewhere less than ideal we could sustain a family on a single income.

Oh, the best laid plans! Here's how the next couple years actually panned out. The market experienced what economic experts referred to as a "double dip," meaning that the "all-time low" at which we had purchased our home went lower still. Our property was soon worth significantly less than what we owed on the mortgage, effectively trapping us there until the market could recover. This second dip in the market had also set off a domino effect of negative consequences: Foreclosures in our area continued to climb, resulting in a large number of folks who were now unable to pay their property taxes. This, in turn, put the city into serious financial straits, leading to a cut of nearly half of the police force. That sudden loss of the presence of law enforcement quickly turned our "poor but safe" neighborhood into a dangerous situation for a young family: drug dealers moving in to set up shop in the unit behind us, gang activity, homeless encampments popping up all along neighboring streets. Suffice it to say, absolutely nothing went as we had planned.

The market did recover eventually, and we were finally able to sell the town house. But after paying off the debt we had accrued during those stints of unemployment, there simply wasn't much money left over for a down payment on a decent Bay Area home—and we had two small children to consider now. We were both beyond exhausted, so when the Holy Spirit began nudging us on that Oregon trip? We were more than ready to listen. What started as mere musing began to evolve into something a bit more tangible. Perhaps we could make some kind of two-year plan and consider a real exit strategy.

As we neared the end of our trip, a series of events were put into motion that to this day I can't fully explain—but I'll try. My parents had accompanied us on this visit, and they had gone out together that morning for a scenic drive. Just before we had planned to meet back up with them for lunch, I got an unexpected call from my mom that went a little something like this: "I just saw the most 'Stephanie' house for sale. It has this wraparound porch and little shutters on all the windows. You just have to come see it. No open house today, but I called the real-estate agent already and we can all tour it in a half hour. Can you come meet us?"

Mama and I have this guilty habit of touring homes for sale that we don't actually have any intention of buying. We get all kinds of ideas to design our "someday" dream homes, and attending open houses is a free way to spend a weekend afternoon (bonus when they have free cookies!). My husband is an absolute saint, and so he lovingly tolerates this eccentricity. He agreed to accompany us on our tour and play the part of the interested home buyer, even though he was anything but that. At best, he figured he could try to view this little caper as "market research," a way to see exactly how much cheaper homes really were in Oregon. Perhaps we could factor that into our possible two-year plan.

The next day over lunch we were sitting in a real-estate agent's office, mortgage preapproval in hand, signing an offer to purchase that very house. No, you didn't skip a paragraph there. The time between those two events was an absolute whirlwind totaling less than 24 hours. We jokingly told folks that we had accidentally bought a house while on vacation, because in some ways we still don't entirely understand how it happened. One minute we were walking through the house, dreaming of a far-off future when we could somehow hope to own a real home like this one, and then suddenly we were asking the agent if he had a mortgage broker we could speak with about the financing.

We sensed the Holy Spirit moving in our hearts, and we knew beyond a shadow of a doubt that God was calling us to take an extraordinary, albeit seemingly crazy, leap of faith. We didn't know if we had enough for a down payment (we did) or if our offer would even be approved (it was). Scariest of all was the fact that we had no clue whatsoever if Bobby's company would approve the request to telecommute so that he could maintain his job from out of state (you guessed it—they did). All we knew for certain was that God was calling us to make the leap and simply trust that He had worked out the details of the landing. So we did the single craziest thing we have ever done: We bought that house and began to plan for the amazing new life in store for us in Oregon.

God was
calling us
to make the
leap and simply
trust that He
had worked out
the details of
the landing.

A Season of Abundance?

Almost as soon as we began to share our news, we started to hear a theme in our friends' responses.

"You guys are so overdue for this."

"I knew God would show up for you like this one day!"

"It's been such a long season for you both. I'm so excited to see you finally get to a place of normalcy after all the trials you've endured."

"That's what happens when you obey in faith! The rewards are always worth the struggle."

The words washed over us like a long-awaited rain after unbearable drought. The truth was, it *had* been a long and difficult season—not only with the financial struggles and times of unemployment, but also with multiple painful miscarriages and two equally painful failed adoption attempts. There had also been two successful but difficult pregnancies that came with numerous complications of their own (including three months of terrifying bed rest trying to keep in my son Jack, who appeared determined to make an early exit), an autism diagnosis after years of questions and struggle with our eldest son, Aidan, and just over a decade of intense chronic pain and seemingly never-ending health problems that my doctors still were trying to diagnose or explain.

At one point we sought counseling to sort through the grief and stress that threatened to tear apart our young marriage, only to be met with the reassurance that we had been pummeled by more in our few years together than many couples with a decade or more between them. "If you've managed to stick it out through all of this," we were told, "I'm willing to wager just about anything that you two are going to make it."

Yes, it had been a long, hard road, and finally the clouds seemed to be parting to let God's favor shine on our weary souls. We were ready to leave this season of "survival mode" behind us and finally live in a newly found season of joy, the way we were sure God intended. We had listened to the urgings of the Spirit and had followed God's leading, and now we were ready with arms open wide to reap His blessings in abundance. As we pulled out of the driveway to start the long journey to our new home, I cried tears of relief and gratitude while blasting Casting Crowns' "Thrive" over the stereo. God had proved faithful indeed, and we were going to gratefully shout our testimonies of His goodness to anyone who would listen.

We had three glorious months in that home before the phone call came. The company my husband worked for was going under, and they were eliminating his job to try to slow the bleeding.

Never had there been so much as a hint that the company was struggling. We were totally blindsided by their call. We were now living in a state with far more limited job opportunities in my husband's field, carrying a brand-new mortgage, and facing the impending termination of our sole source of income. And the hits just kept coming.

When my husband went to apply for unemployment benefits to help tide us over while he looked for work, we discovered that a tiny typo was all it took to throw our life deeper into chaos. His former employer had made a single digit error on his W-2 form, right in the middle of his social security number. This effectively created a clerical nightmare in which California had no record of us paying into unemployment, as all those paycheck deductions had been associated with a different social security number entirely. There would be no checks coming anytime soon. We were on our own.

For three and a half long months we were not only without a full-time paycheck, but without any income at all. We had spent whatever savings we once had on the down payment for our home as

well as the enormous costs of moving out of state. In short, we had
nothing left to fall back on, and we watched Bobby's last paycheck
dwindle into nothing while he desperately searched for a new job to
support us. Our mortgage was soon in default, and our home was
at very real risk of foreclosure. We were dependent on a combination of food stamps and supernatural provision to provide for even
our basic needs. Our first winter in our new state was proving to be
a harsh and difficult one. Where was the season of abundance we
had been told to expect?

··

Where was the season of abundance we had been told to expect?

··

It was there, in the middle of this dark winter season, that we
received the surprise of our life. What had started as a stomach bug
had developed into two weeks of nausea and then into two little
blue lines staring back at my disbelieving face. We were expecting.
You could have knocked me over with a single breath. This was *not*
something we had even remotely planned for. Could there possibly be a worse time for this news? How did this even happen? And
why was it happening now? How on earth were we ever going to
afford this?

It took a couple weeks for me to wrestle with my fears, but
slowly my anxieties were eclipsed by the instinctual bond between
a mother and her child. Each day I fell more head over heels in love
with this unexpected little miracle in my womb. She became the
glorious light in a season of so much darkness, an anchor of hope for
my storm-tossed soul. Yes, she had been anything but planned, but

I grew to fervently believe that the arrival of this little one was just another way God was going to show Himself not only to me, but to anyone who would see our story unfold. We had already seen Him use the incredible story of our son Jack, who had beaten so many odds to fight his way into his miraculous existence, and I assumed this new blessing would be the same: a testimony to serve as another example of God's unending faithfulness.

I was equal parts nerves and excitement as I chatted with the OB while she prepped the ultrasound at my appointment. We shared a laugh over just how much babies don't seem to care about our best laid plans or our ideal timing. We briefly reviewed my pregnancy history, and she was quick to put me at ease with some anecdotes about how previous miscarriages don't reliably predict future pregnancy outcomes.

But then the words came: "I'm so sorry." I was blindsided, as if a tidal wave had broken over me with no warning at all. I felt the air leave my lungs as I was pulled under by each word she spoke. "Not viable." Time seemed to stop. I found myself desperately scanning the walls for a clock, unable to maintain eye contact with the face across from me. "No heartbeat."

I grew increasingly aggravated. *Why isn't there a clock in this room? How do they expect people to keep track of the time if they don't have a clock in here?* The OB continued, "We can give it a couple more days, but I'd like to go ahead and schedule the procedure, just to be on the safe side." *Procedure?* I had clearly missed something in my frantic search for the nonexistent clock.

"Missed miscarriage." "D and C." "Outpatient procedure." I tried to focus on her words, but my brain only processed a scarce and scattered few. I still felt like I was drowning, yet somehow like I was also dying of thirst. *Didn't I bring a water bottle?*

"Do you have any questions?" All I had were questions. Why

didn't they have a clock? Why on earth had I told my husband he could skip this routine appointment? Where was my water bottle? How could my body somehow miss the memo that this pregnancy was over? Where was the telltale cramping and bleeding that had always marked my miscarriages? Why would God put me through this heart-wrenching pain yet again? I have no memory of scheduling the D and C procedure. I don't have any recollection of leaving that examination room. I don't know for certain how I got across the parking lot to my car. I can only assume that I walked. Somehow, I remember that it was raining. I don't actually remember calling my husband with the news—or any part of what I said. I still wonder how long I sat in that parking lot before driving myself home, and I can't picture any of the drive. All of it is a blur, as if the files in my brain holding the memories of that day were somehow corrupted. Perhaps the pain was so unbearable that my mind simply didn't record them to begin with. The only memory I can see clearly is me lying on my bathroom floor, curled up in the fetal position around the womb that had once again betrayed me, with my tear-streaked face uncomfortably stuck to the cold linoleum floor. It was all I could do to cry out from that floor with the same repeated lament, "I don't understand, God. I just don't understand."

We had taken the extraordinary leap of faith, without question or delay. We had been obedient when He asked us to leave everything we knew and head off like Abraham for a new life in a new land. We had been faithful to share our testimony of His goodness to us. We went to church, read our Bibles, hosted community groups, and raised our children to love Jesus. We tithed faithfully, even when it hurt. We were doing everything we knew how, and yet here we were again. Broken. Devastated. Empty-handed.

It was there on my bathroom floor, in a state of utter broken-ness, that God started to sow the seeds of healing. Amid all the uncertainty and chaos, all my broken dreams and unmet expectations, He quietly began to draw me closer to His heart. When everything else had been stripped away, and I held those empty hands out to Him, begging for anything I could hold on to, it was then He showed me the height, depth, and breadth of His unending love for me.

In the days and weeks that followed I began to bury myself in the Word, hoping to find answers to why these trials seemed to be never ending. Why was there so much suffering and heartache? How could a loving God allow so much pain in the life of someone earnestly striving to serve Him? How was any of this fair? Were these the attacks of Satan? Or was God trying to teach me some lesson that I just wasn't grasping yet and was doomed to repeat endlessly until I could? When would we finally get past all the struggling and get back to something resembling a normal life?

Almost immediately in my searching, one point became painfully clear. God was about to tear down this idea of a normal life piece by piece and replace it with an unexpected change in perspective. I had come to Him seeking the reasons for my specific trials, hoping He would show me just enough details of His perfect plan to make it easier for me to understand His will. If I knew where He was taking me and why, it would be that much easier for me to accept His plans.

Little did I realize He had no intention of showing me His road map. No, He wanted to teach me how to trust Him enough to have total peace, even when I can't make out the road ahead. He didn't want me to look for the proof of how His goodness would unfold; He wanted to show me how to see His unchanging goodness in the midst of the pain. He was teaching my heart to let go of all my most fervently held assumptions, come to Him in total surrender, and genuinely proclaim, "If not, You are still good."

I had found my rock bottom, and instead of pulling me out of the broken pieces of my shattered expectations, the God of the universe met me there in the rubble. Inside my grief I found the start of a deepening intimacy with God that I had never known possible. There was something sacred in the pain, as if somehow, in this suffering, I was standing on holy ground, breathtakingly close to the great I Am. From that holy rubble He was building something new, with passion and purpose growing from deep within the fertile ground below. God was about to replace all my carefully laid plans and great expectations with His perfect best—something so far beyond anything I ever thought I wanted and everything I never knew I needed.

Chapter 2

The Default State

Life is pain. Anybody that says different is selling something.

WILLIAM GOLDMAN[1]

W hen a friend of mine received a difficult diagnosis, she chose to share it on Facebook as she tried to process her feelings. She was grappling with her new reality: At barely 21 years of age she had a chronic, incurable condition, one that meant coping with daily pain and a gradually worsening disability for the rest of her life. Understandably, she was reaching out to friends and loved ones online for support as she struggled with the news.

As I scrolled down to leave some words of encouragement on her post, one particular comment jumped out and grabbed my attention: "Don't speak that over yourself. You do not have fibromyalgia! I rebuke that in the name of Jesus! God wants you well. Speak healing over yourself."

As much as I was taken aback by the post, I really shouldn't have been. This was a sentiment I had heard so many times in my own 15-year struggle with chronic pain and disability. In fact, just the day before I read that post, a well-meaning connection had sent me an email suggesting I should listen to an online sermon on disease and healing. The message description includes the following statement: "[Religion] even tries to make us believe that sickness is a

25

blessing. That's just not true. God wants you well."[2] In the sermon, the preacher points to stories of Jesus healing the blind and calling the lame to rise up and walk, and he claims emphatically that the New Testament offers an undeniable precedent that Jesus would always heal anyone who truly asks for it, and the healing would always be immediate and complete. He goes on to explain that Jesus had instantly defeated all earthly diseases by His death on the cross, a belief he supports almost entirely with a single line from a single verse: "With his wounds we are healed" (Isaiah 53:5).

It's appealing, to be sure, the idea that a believer in Christ need never experience earthly pain or disease and has only to call upon the name of Jesus to receive instant relief. Didn't Jesus heal the sick? Doesn't He want only the very best for His children? Aren't we taught that every good and perfect gift comes from our Father above (James 1:17)? All those other "gifts"—the issues and problems that hurt us—those could only come from the enemy, right?

It would seem logical, then, to conclude that disease and suffering are just spiritual attacks meant to keep us from being fully effective ministers of the gospel. Or perhaps they are punishment for sins of which we have not repented, the penalty for displeasing a perfect and holy God. Either way, they are an obstacle to be overcome and defeated, and surely Scripture must hold the key to moving beyond what ails us and brings us pain.

However, this seemingly logical conclusion, this theology of wellness and prosperity gifted from a God who only seeks to see us healthy and flourishing and living without pain, is not biblical. Not even a little bit. In fact, the deeper we dive into what Scripture really says about suffering, the more we discover that not only did God never promise us those things on this side of eternity, but He lovingly guides us away from the pursuit of earthly happiness. Instead, He sets us on a path to becoming ever more like Christ. He strips away the expectations of a "normal life" and replaces them with an open-handed surrender to an extraordinary life lived in intimacy and dependence on the God who saves. He breaks down our idols of security and ease and leads us lovingly to the feet of a God who's making us more like Himself while stripping away all our attachments to this earthly shell.

I don't want to downplay how difficult this mental shift really is. It would be disingenuous to pretend that this requires anything less than a complete transformation and renewal of our minds. It would be so much easier to avoid this topic of suffering altogether, to simply rejoice with those who rejoice and gloss over all the pesky references to those who mourn. It's far easier to share stories of provision and abundance and proclaim, "See, God is faithful," than to look into our vulnerable, broken places or to sit with those who are hurting and ask, "But where is God now?"

Yet the difficult subject of pain is ultimately inextricable from any desire to know God more intimately. The theology of suffering goes right to the heart of our relationship with God in the temporal realm. Suffering is the one universal experience that ties each of us horizontally to one another and vertically to Christ, because each and every one of us experiences pain, disease, and heartache in this mortal life—Christ Himself not excepted. There is not one of us who can say we've enjoyed a life free of suffering, nor will there ever be someone who can. It's the universal unifier.

Before we go any further, I want to offer a warning of sorts: In order to build up a new and glorious understanding, we first have to tear down much of what we've already constructed in our minds. Much like a remodeling project, we've got to go through the uncomfortable process of smashing down walls and ripping out fixtures, living inside the dust and debris while the painstaking phase of rebuilding begins. This process of stripping away old comforts and faulty theologies and facing the realities of our broken world is painful, and you may finish this chapter feeling somewhat battered and bruised. But here's the good news: We already know the ending, and it's glorious. Jesus wins, we are not left forsaken, and the new thing He's going to build far surpasses anything we must let go of in the meantime. In the book of John, Jesus promises, "In the world you will have tribulation. But take heart; I have overcome the world" (John 16:33). While this chapter ultimately deals with the first half of the verse, take heart: There are so many better things to come.

No Surprise

First Peter is an excellent place to start when looking to lay a foundation for a biblical perspective on suffering: "Beloved, do not be surprised at the fiery trial when it comes upon you to test you, as though something strange were happening to you" (4:12). To give you a little background, this is a letter that was written to the church in Asia Minor, a church that was struggling under a nearly constant onslaught of persecution and painful circumstances. Peter, the writer, consistently weaves the theme of suffering throughout the epistle, yet we never read any exhortations to rebuke suffering—rather, he says to expect trials to come.

"Do not be surprised," the apostle tells them. With these four small words we begin to sense that our cultural view of suffering as a surprising detour from our normal lives isn't going to coexist easily with Scripture. We open with four little words that pack a sledgehammer-like force of destruction to our expectations and our very notions of normalcy. Isn't our most visceral reaction to tragedy one of shock? "This can't be happening," we say to ourselves. We comfort our neighbors in crisis with the words, "I just can't believe this happened to you," or, "How could this happen to such wonderful people?" Yet the apostle tells us, "Do not be surprised." This admonition seems to defy our logic.

Let's keep going.

"Do not be surprised at the fiery trial when it comes upon you." Notice he doesn't say "if," but rather "when." I always like to underline words like this when I'm reading Scripture, words that are seemingly small and could be easily overlooked in a quick read but greatly affect the message of the text and could alter the whole meaning if they were changed. The word *when* here is that sort of word. Do not be surprised *when* your fiery trial comes. The message is inescapable: The trials will come. It's just a matter of when.

This may be the most difficult idea we'll wrestle with, and yet it also has to be the first—the very foundation on which all the other truths about suffering will be built. Suffering *will* happen. Tragedy *will* strike. Trials *will* come. None of this should be surprising to us because it is an entirely unavoidable facet of the human experience. None of us will escape this life without scars. In fact, Peter again echoes the sentiment at the end of the verse, "Do not be surprised...as though something strange were happening to you." Our suffering is not a strange occurrence or an unexpected detour from the normal path of life. There isn't a secret method we can unlock to avoid the pitfalls and navigate through life unscathed. Life will be marked by painful experiences no matter what we do. In this broken and fallen world, suffering isn't the exception to the rule—it's the default state of being.

This difficult truth is all too often missing from our modern theology. Life in our day and age is marked by a relentless pursuit of comfort and security, and the church is not immune to this cultural shift. At one extreme, the so-called "prosperity gospel" has rapidly grown in popularity and reach through numerous television

programs, radio broadcasts, and works of Christian nonfiction that
have been elevated to the top of the best-seller lists.

Yet it's a mistake to assume that as long as we rebuke the obviously false teachers promising mansions and private planes, we have
escaped the prosperity gospel's reach. Many mainstream Christians
who decry the more obvious teachings of "wealth, health, and prosperity" have unknowingly let a large amount of prosperity-gospel
influence slip into their own theologies. How many of us believe,
on some level, that God directly rewards the good behavior of
believers with earthly blessings? How many of us believe that, if we
walk in obedience to God's command, we have tapped into a secret
holy conduit that will help us avoid earthly suffering? We may not
believe in a literal formula that converts our tithing into a clear-cut
financial return on investment, yet how often do we convince ourselves that we have otherwise purchased His favor with our obedience and good behavior? How often is our gut reaction to hard
times to cry out, "But God, I don't understand—I'm doing what
You asked of me!" How often do we lay out our case for why we
don't seemingly deserve the painful trial we find ourselves facing?
"But I serve faithfully in my church!" or, "But I'm raising up my
children in the Word!" or, "But I don't party or use drugs!" or, "But
I'm always grateful for my blessings and make sure to tell everyone
about Your faithfulness!"

It's always in our times of greatest suffering that our core beliefs
are most exposed. When we react to tragedy and pain with a sense of
disbelief, a feeling of betrayal, or an urge to lay out a defense for why
we simply don't deserve these painful circumstances, we can see just
how much we have bought into the idea of some sort of heavenly
ledger that holds our good deeds in account and ultimately deter-
mines how deserving we are of reward or pain.

Clinging to Our Works

Belief in the prosperity gospel is not always characterized by the stereotypical sense of entitlement to financial wealth; it is far more commonly expressed in the sincerely held belief that making good choices will guarantee a certain level of security and reward. All too often, modern theology is infected by the idolization of independence and personal responsibility. We convince ourselves that we can control our own destiny and almost entirely lose sight of our dependence on the Creator. We begin to claim credit for His provision for us: If we are granted good health, it is because we ate the right food or avoided bad habits; if we are given financial security, it is because we worked hard and made wise investments. We may admit that our salvation is by grace alone, but we desperately cling to our works in all other areas.

One of the biggest problems with adopting these prosperity-gospel ideas into the way we view ourselves is that our personal theology will always inform the ways we view others and behave toward them as well. It's impossible to separate what we believe from the actions it ultimately inspires. When I adopt a system of belief that says my financial prosperity is the reward for behaving a certain way, the inevitable conclusion to that way of thinking is that people experiencing poverty simply need to make better choices and they, too, could enjoy this same prosperity. When I believe that I'm physically healthy and able bodied because of my wise choices or because I'm receiving an earthly reward for my spiritual obedience, such logic ends with a belief that people who are sick or disabled have either made poor decisions or, in more extreme cases, are perhaps being punished for sin in their life. In John 9, for example, the disciples come upon a man who was born blind and immediately ask Jesus, "Who sinned, this man or his parents?" (verse 2). When we corrupt our own theology with prosperity-gospel thinking, it's simply impossible for that belief not to bleed into the way we view and behave toward others.

The ongoing political debates about health care provide a perfect example of how this seemingly personal belief actually informs and influences the way we view and treat one another. This issue hits especially close to home for my family, as access to quality health insurance is the only way we are able to maintain access to the many medications, specialists, and lifelong therapies that my medical conditions require. Some of these issues are potentially fatal without ongoing medical care, meaning that health insurance is quite literally a life-and-death issue for me.

With that in mind, try to imagine how I felt when I was sitting in on a discussion about health care with other believers in Christ, and a gentleman began to repeat an analogy that had been presented by a lawmaker on television the day before. "Forcing insurance companies to insure sick people with preexisting conditions," he told our group, "is like asking a car insurance company to sell you insurance for a vehicle that's been totaled in an accident already." His quip was like a punch to the gut—a brother in Christ nonchalantly comparing my life to a wrecked car that should be taken to the dump and disposed of for parts. You may hear this story and picture a generally rude and unloving person, but this was someone I had always respected. This was a passionate Jesus follower, a beacon of faith, and a wonderful husband and father. When confronted with how deeply devaluing and cutting these words were for someone like myself, his response was something I will never be able to forget. "Don't make it so personal," he said. "This is just about politics; it's not meant to be applied to you personally. It's just supposed to be a big-picture conversation."

I tell you this story to illustrate two very important points.

First, the way we choose to view our fellow human beings is always personal. There is simply no way to discuss the big-picture ideas of politics, or the seemingly personal beliefs that inform our political views, without affecting real human beings on the other end. While it is wise to caution against letting our politics influence our faith, it's impossible to think our faith does not influence our politics. Far too often we buy into the lie that people of faith should never be political, and cries of "we should stop fighting about politics and just get along" are commonly heard in our faith communities. While we are certainly called to avoid *partisanship*, it's impossible to avoid *politics*. Politics isn't simply the machinations of a small, powerful elite in Washington, DC; politics is ultimately the way we define what we owe to our neighbors and what kind of community we have chosen to be. Politics is always about real people. So in our desire to foster unity in the body of Christ, let us be careful not to silence those suffering in our midst behind cries of "don't take it personally."

Second, this story serves as a tangible, real-life example of how unchecked prosperity-gospel theologies are aggressive roots from which a toxic worldview can grow in the heart of even the most faithful and well-meaning Christian. If we believe that our physical health is earned through our wise choices or faithful Christian obedience, or that total healing from all physical disease is promised to any good believer who simply exercises enough faith in the asking, it's only inevitable that we would, by extension, feel less responsible for providing for anyone's medical care. If we believe that our personal financial prosperity is something we rightfully earned by our choices alone, we will inevitably view the poor as lacking our level of wisdom, faith, and determination—and then we might feel justified in leaving them to reap the negative consequences we are sure they have brought on themselves.

This conversation about a theology of suffering is more vital than ever to the body of Christ. We cannot be lulled into complacency by the ubiquitous idea that the prosperity gospel is only really damaging when there are televangelists with private planes and multimillion-dollar mansions manipulating retirement accounts away from unwitting senior citizens.

Satan is smart, and one of his most insidious tactics is to give us an easily identifiable extreme to focus on so that we don't see the less obvious roots of the very same sin in our own life. The essential truth is that if we cannot learn to correctly identify and root out prosperity-gospel beliefs hidden within our own hearts, they will silently infect and corrupt our theology until it poisons our witness and renders us ineffective messengers of the gospel. The way we understand suffering, and our ability to see it as a universal aspect of the human experience, is fundamental to being able to truly love our neighbors as we love ourselves. Perhaps Father Gregory Boyle put it best when he said, "If you're a stranger to your own wound, then you're gonna be tempted to despise the wounded."[3]

· ·

The way we understand suffering, and our ability to see it as a universal aspect of the human experience, is fundamental to being able to truly love our neighbors as we love ourselves.

· ·

Peek back a few pages to read the very first word of the "do not be surprised" verse (1 Peter 4:12). Did you catch that? *Beloved.* A proper theology of suffering naturally aligns us more closely with God's heart for our fellow humans and cultivates a deep and authentic love for those who are suffering in our midst. Peter calls these believers not just his friends, or even brothers and sisters, but his "beloved." This is the heart and soul of why we must commit to grappling with these hard and holy concepts, and why the theology of suffering must be seen as an essential piece of our spiritual formation. It is only when we learn to expect our own suffering to inevitably and unavoidably come that we can authentically empathize with the suffering of others, and we can wholly belong to each other as "beloved."

Destined to Suffer

Peter isn't the only New Testament writer to explore the theology of suffering in his letters. The writings of the apostle Paul are crucial to any biblical exploration of suffering. It is anything but surprising that Paul spent a great deal of his letters on themes of suffering, because his own experiences gave him such a deep familiarity with pain and persecution. He spent so much of his ministry being chased off, threatened, beaten, and literally held captive in chains that his words have an added layer of authority and credibility. You will never be tempted to think, *Well, that's easy for you to say*, when it comes to Paul.

In 1 Thessalonians, Paul wrote to the church in Thessalonica, a bustling metropolis in Macedonia. Thanks to an account of Paul's ministry in the book of Acts, we know that his time spent bringing the gospel to this city had been rather brief (see Acts 17:2) before Paul fled Thessalonica and headed for Berea. This left a large church of relatively new believers, most of whom were Gentiles, without the physical presence of Paul there to guide them. Unfortunately for the Thessalonians, they also had virtually no time after their conversion before they faced enormous persecution of their own, and this quite understandably left many of them wrestling with their new beliefs. Paul writes to the church here both to help strengthen their battered faith and to offer some perspective on their difficult circumstances.

In the beginning of the letter, we see Paul expressing his deep affection for this particular body of believers, while almost immediately acknowledging the difficult circumstances this church faced from the very beginning (1 Thessalonians 1:6; 2:14-15). He's clearly proud of them for choosing to follow Jesus, especially in light of very real persecution, but he also recognizes how difficult this could be for them, given their young faith. Paul writes how much he longs to be there to lead and comfort them in person, but how that simply isn't possible at the time (2:17-18). He explains that he has sent Timothy in his place, in order "to establish and exhort you in your faith, that no one be moved by these afflictions. For you yourselves know that we are destined for this" (3:2-3). Now bear with me for a minute, because I don't want us to miss the enormous truth buried here in a seemingly small turn of phrase. To fully grasp Paul's statement, we need to take a look at the Greek.

The phrase I want us to home in on is "we are *destined* for this" (3:3, emphasis added). The word *destined* immediately caught my attention, as *destiny* is usually up there with *karma* in the lexicon of words Christians avoid like the plague. So down the rabbit hole I went to see if I could get any additional insights into what Paul had really said. The Greek used here is *keimetha* (κείμεθα), from the word *keimai* (κεῖμαι). The word has a few definitions, but it's typically used to communicate either being appointed to a special position or role (like being appointed to be the mayor or a city councillor) or being made for a specific purpose or goal (like making a law to address a specific need or laying down bricks to make a road).[4]

Don't miss this: Paul is telling this battered body of new believers not to be shaken by either Paul's persecution or by their own afflictions. Why? Because this is their holy destiny. They were appointed to this anointed role, set apart by God, and perfectly designed to withstand the very struggles they now face.

In this seemingly small turn of phrase, Paul flips the entire premise of the prosperity gospel on its head. The idea that our suffering is either a detour from or an obstacle to our walk with God is torn away, and we are given instead a radical new understanding of what it means to choose to follow Jesus. Expect suffering. Do not be surprised when the fiery trial comes, because you can rest assured in the knowledge that you were created for this. You were designed for this holy purpose. This isn't a mistake, a detour, or a punishment. You were appointed to this holy calling, so you know you won't be shaken or moved by it. You were made for this.

In fact, if we flip back to 1 Peter, we will see this same sentiment echoed in that letter as well: "If when you do good and suffer for it you endure, this is a gracious thing in the sight of God. For to this *you have been called*, because Christ also suffered for you, leaving you an example, so that you might follow in his steps" (1 Peter 2:20-21, emphasis added).

These are two letters written by two different authors to two very different churches, both of which were experiencing the common thread of suffering despite their very genuine and active faiths in Jesus Christ. In both cases the author comforts his readers not by telling them how to shake off their trials and return to their callings, but instead by reassuring them that their suffering itself is a calling—one they were perfectly designed for. They aren't told that more closely following Jesus can help them avoid pain here on earth, but rather that the very decision to follow after Jesus leads to walking in the steps of His very real suffering.

There's a temptation here to interpret this idea as saying, "God causes me to suffer to cause my growth." I want to be clear: That's not at all what we're talking about here. It's a difficult nuance to grapple with, but there is a big difference in saying, "God gave me cancer," and saying, "God takes the things intended for our harm—even cancer—and uses them for our benefit." When we talk about being destined for this, we aren't saying that God created humanity with the intention of sending us disease and persecution and poverty and death because He wanted to refine us to be more like Him. There are certainly those who are teaching that message, and I want to say as emphatically as possible that I am not one of them. I am speaking here of an all-knowing God who saw all of time before it began, who knew this perfect world He would create would one day see sin and darkness corrupt it, and who perfectly designed each and every one of us not only to withstand our suffering, but to somehow benefit from it. It's almost beyond comprehension: a God so powerful that He can take the darkness and pain He never wished this world to contain and still somehow use it for His purposes and our benefit.

These are hard ideas to wrestle with, but the most sacred truths usually are. I would question any theology of something as complex as suffering and pain that doesn't leave us feeling pulled in seemingly conflicting directions. Holy questions rarely have simple answers. Whether it's Paul writing of his mental struggle between grace and the law, or the modern church grappling to find a balance between speaking truth and showing love, the most sacred beliefs exist in tension. It's when we choose the more comfortable option of picking a side and wrapping it up neatly in an easily explainable bow that we really start to get it wrong. The theology of suffering is no exception. Don't rush to try to resolve that tension. Sit in that discomfort. Let it stand as proof that we serve a God not created by human minds, but One who is beyond our human comprehension or explanation.

~

Holy
questions
rarely have
simple
answers.

~

With that in mind, let's go back into Peter's letter to look at one more verse: "Let those who suffer according to God's will entrust their souls to a faithful Creator while doing good" (1 Peter 4:19). Once again there is a temptation to read the phrase "who suffer according to God's will" and interpret that as "God causes suffering." That's an inaccurate interpretation not only of what Peter is saying in his letter, but also of who we know God to be. The idea of God reaching down to purposefully give cancer to a small child or to widow a young mother-to-be simply doesn't reflect a just or loving God. But what else could Peter have meant here, and how can this verse be seen in any way as encouragement to those who are suffering?

Let's return again to our earlier picture of an all-knowing God who exists outside the confines of time and who was able to perfectly create each and every one of us with the ability to not only withstand the suffering He knew would come our way, but also to be able to benefit from that which brings us harm. In the latter half of this verse, Peter encourages these believers with the truth that they can "entrust their souls to a faithful Creator." Of all the words to use for God here, Peter chooses to refer to Him as Creator and includes the important descriptor of *faithful* as well. He reminds these believers that they were created by a faithful and perfect Father who knew everything before time began and who intentionally made them exactly who they would need to be to walk out the callings before them. Where Peter says, "According to God's will," I see a reminder to the believers that nothing that comes against them ever has the power to disrupt the perfect plans of God, and that nothing that befalls them is either surprising to Him or beyond what He has created them to be able to bear. Peter isn't saying, "God is doing this to you," but rather, "His plans for you will not be and cannot be in any way disrupted by this. Trust that He faithfully created you with everything you need to face this—because He has always known it would come."

⌒

Is your heart feeling a bit heavy after all that? I can imagine you thinking, *Basically, you're telling me the Bible says my life's going to be terrible, so I should just start to expect that and give up hope now? Gee, thanks.* Trust me, when I first began to study these passages, there were many nights I wanted to throw my Bible across the room and scream. You might be reading this as you walk through your own journey of pain, grief, heartache, or loss. I know you might be wondering how anyone could find a shred of hope, let alone a life of joy, with a theology like this. I think it's important to share a few words of encouragement here that I don't want you to miss.

First, the hardest part is now behind you, and it only gets better from here. I promise. Remember the picture of the remodeling project? In that analogy, you're currently sitting on a rough plywood subfloor; you have no stove or running water; and you can barely breathe through the thick sawdust air as the shredded remnants of tile and cabinets lie in piles around you. This is not the time to fire your contractor and try to scrape the tattered pieces of your old kitchen back together. Hold on to the promise of how much better it's going to be in the end.

I won't only leave you with the promise of what is to come, though. There's hope to be found even in what we've tackled so far. As hard as it is to confront the idea that suffering is an inescapable facet of the human experience, there is an enormous amount of peace to be found right there inside that same truth. It means you can let go of the shame or fear that you've done something wrong to bring suffering into your life. Let go of the lies that whisper, "Maybe God is punishing you," or, "Maybe you didn't have enough faith."

After one of our most painful miscarriages, I spent a horrific amount of time studying an Old Testament story in which a baby's death is said to be the result of the parent's sin (2 Samuel 12). I would cry out to God, begging Him to reveal whatever it was He was punishing me for with so many miscarriages. I would sit in church on Sunday and wonder, *Do I not have enough faith that He can give me a living child? Are my doubts what are keeping these prayers from being answered?* It was only when I began to understand that suffering is universal, even among the most obedient of Christians with the sincerest of faiths, that I was able to unchain myself from the heavy burden of shame, guilt, and self-blame.

Remember, dear friend, you were faithfully created by a God who has equipped you to do hard and holy things. Whatever your pain, whatever unspeakable grief you are enduring right now, whatever unfulfilled longing continues to weigh heavy on your heart, there is nothing that can separate you from the love of God or disrupt His perfect plans for your life everlasting. Whatever temporal pain you may experience, it will ultimately be eclipsed by eternal glory (2 Corinthians 4:17). Do not be surprised when your suffering comes or let shame whisper lies of blame into your heart, but rest in the knowledge that you were made for this—and you will not be defeated by it.

Chapter 3

Turn Your Eyes

Most of us find it very difficult to want "Heaven" at all—except in so far as "Heaven" means meeting again our friends who have died. One reason for this difficulty is that we have not been trained: our whole education tends to fix our minds on this world.

C.S. Lewis[1]

H ow many children do you have?"
It's an innocent question commonly posed to most every mother, and yet each time I'm asked, my breath catches in my throat. I've learned to cope well enough over the years, usually responding, "Right now, we have two boys," and dutifully listing off names and ages. But in my mind, I always struggle through the same unspoken responses. The truth, of course, is that I'm the mother of nine, though my family fits comfortably in a four-seater car. Yet the world is simply not prepared for its basic social niceties to be interrupted with a painful recounting of the saga of our seven miscarriages. "Right now, we have two boys," I'll respond, so the conversation continues its cadence without pause; only my heart secretly lingers behind to reflect and remember.

All nine of my children have names, each one carefully chosen with special consideration for its meaning. I've always felt that naming a child is a sacred undertaking to be considered thoughtfully, and researching the meanings of names and their cultural roots has always been a part of my process. We've often joked that we took a great risk naming our firstborn son Aidan, which means "little fire," as we certainly didn't know if that fire would end up burning us in the end! His brother Jack's name was actually picked entirely for its meaning—"God is gracious"—a name chosen in gratitude and recognition of the gracious God who knew that our hearts needed the unique infusion of joy this miraculous little boy brought to some of our darkest places.

There are seven other names, though. Seven names that were never painstakingly hand-lettered across the cover of a baby book. Seven names never piped in frosting across a birthday cake. Seven names never penned on the tags of school jackets, proudly scrawled out in crayon on artwork attached to the refrigerator, printed across diplomas or wedding invitations, or signed on the bottom of Mother's Day cards. There are seven names that were never heralded on social media with birth weights and delivery times and photos of an exhausted mother bursting with love and pride as she shares the first photos of her precious new arrival. There are seven names that live in the pregnant pause of each new breath I draw in, lingering deep in my chest, only to exit again in a silent exhalation from lips that can't seem to form around their sounds.

- Nathaniel means "God's gift."
- Gabriel means "God is my strength."
- Ava means "life."
- Hannah means "grace of God."
- Timothy means "honoring God."
- Noah means "comfort."
- Karis means "grace."

Each one of these precious names was chosen after I had been left not only with an empty womb, but empty arms as well. So why do it? Why break my heart into pieces, agonizingly searching through names and their meanings to choose ones for children who would never need them? There were no birth certificates or even headstones to write them on, so what possible purpose could be served in these names other than to create lasting reminders of pain that most anyone would want to forget?

I named each and every one of these little ones to remind me of two sacred truths, truths that ultimately held me together in the midst of unspeakable grief.

First, choosing names is an intentional and lasting reminder that these children exist. A name serves as a proclamation of their personhood, a signpost of sorts to declare that each one of these children is a real person. Each one is a human soul intentionally knit together by the God of the universe and imprinted with a piece of His very image, which He gave us the sacred opportunity to see reflected within them. This reason alone makes each one of these children deserving of their individual name, but there was something more—something that would uniquely shape my theology of suffering with each name we added to this tear-soaked list. These names forever remind me that heaven is real, and my children are there. Each name paints a clearer picture of the restoration that will come when my once-empty arms will enfold this huge gaggle of children all at once.

I won't pretend to have all the answers as to why seven of my children never drew their first breath on earth. I won't tell you that "everything happens for a reason," as if the depths of human suffering could all be explained on a single bumper sticker. I certainly won't dishonor or disregard the personhood of these children by claiming that God stole the first breath from their lungs just so I could understand Him more clearly. I don't believe any of those things are true. What I can say, though, with the most earnest sincerity and with the peace that defies all human understanding, is that in time I was able to find the goodness buried deep inside unspeakable wrong. I am still able to emphatically say that my loving God didn't want this to happen to anyone, and had this world never fallen into brokenness and sin, I am confident that miscarriage would never have entered the picture. And I can somehow say with equal confidence that He has used even this for my good.

These are two seemingly contradictory ideas, and it can feel impossible for our human brain to reconcile them. But again, I would urge us to sit squarely inside this tension without rushing to seek to resolve it. That tension points to a God who was not created by human minds, and so our most sacred truths are almost never simplistic and easy to digest. Losing seven of my nine children could never be seen as "good," and I don't think God is asking me to believe that. Yet, somehow, there has been so much goodness inextricably mingled with one of the deepest pains I have ever known.

Longing for Heaven

One of those treasures of good God brought forth from that grief was this: Losing these seven children created a permanent longing for heaven inside me, and each new loss gave me a deepening perspective on eternity that I'm unsure I could have grasped with such clarity any other way. When I began to press into my study of biblical suffering, it became clear that this altered perception wasn't somehow unique to my own experiences with pain and grief. In fact, Scripture would lead me to believe that the way tragedy triggers this eternal perspective shift is a gift God deliberately encoded into each of us.

Tragedy shakes
us from our
routine with
unavoidable
force, pushing us
to reexamine
the foundational
truths we
otherwise ignore.

This became the first tangible example God showed me of a truth we discussed in our last chapter: Our all-knowing God not only equipped us to survive the suffering He knew would enter our world, but He also specifically designed us to be able to benefit from what is meant to harm us. He deliberately fashioned the human soul in such a way that, instead of the distance Satan most certainly hoped suffering would create between ourselves and our Creator, suffering could connect us to Him more deeply. Because of this perfect design, our pain has the ability to shift our perspective profoundly, more than any other human experience. Tragedy shakes us from our routine with unavoidable force, pushing us to reexamine the foundational truths we otherwise ignore. In a world increasingly full of distractions, our suffering becomes a distinct opportunity to step outside the routine of our schedule, our accomplishments, our home, our social network, and our plans. It asks us to confront the uncomfortable truth we too often miss: "This world is not our home" (Hebrews 13:14 TLB).

Life in the Tent

Paul conveys this point beautifully in a passage from his second letter to the Corinthians:

> We know that if the tent that is our earthly home is destroyed, we have a building from God, a house not made with hands, eternal in the heavens. For in this tent we groan, longing to put on our heavenly dwelling, if indeed by putting it on we may not be found naked. For while we are still in this tent, we groan, being burdened—not that we would be unclothed, but that we would be further clothed, so that what is mortal may be swallowed up by life. He who has prepared us for this very thing is God, who has given us the Spirit as a

guarantee. So we are always of good courage. We know that while we are at home in the body we are away from the Lord, for we walk by faith, not by sight. Yes, we are of good courage, and we would rather be away from the body and at home with the Lord (5:1-8).

Here we find Paul writing to the church in Corinth, illustrating the tension between yet another pair of seemingly contradictory truths. In this letter, Paul uses the image of a tent to portray concepts about our physical body and our life here on earth. In our modern context, it's easy to refer to a tent as an example of a brutally uncomfortable temporary dwelling, one we may use out of sheer necessity, but all the while seeking to get back home to a warm shower and a real bed. It might seem, then, to be logical to read Paul's words as though he were saying, "Human existence is an awful and fleeting stop on our way to our real home in heaven, so let's just get out of here as fast as we can!" Yet, when we consider a bit of the cultural context of the day, the picture that emerges is far more complex and reveals a deeper set of truths about our time here on earth.

Paul wrote this particular letter to a church in Corinth, a burgeoning cultural metropolis that was flourishing under Roman rule. The people receiving Paul's letter would have lived an urban life, spending their days in city dwellings with some of the more modern amenities of the day. Although tents were not the most common primary home in this culture, like one would see in many of the nomadic cultures of Old Testament stories, tents were still usually much more than a basic temporary shelter from the elements. When tents were set up for long travel, they were essentially large temporary houses, often complete with rugs and furniture and much of the comforts of home. The original readers of Paul's letter could just as easily have been picturing something akin to "glamping" in an Airstream trailer than some rain-soaked Boy Scouts huddled together in an A-frame shelter made by draping a tarp over a stick.

What does this mean for Paul's analogy? Let's try walking through the passage with this more comfortable image of a tent in mind.

In 2 Corinthians 5:1, Paul comforts the Corinthians with the reminder that if our "tent"—meaning our earthly body—is destroyed, we still have an eternal body awaiting us in heaven. Not only does he remind us that our heavenly body is eternal, but he makes sure to acknowledge that the eternal body is far superior to this form here on earth, perfectly designed by our Creator without any of the damaging effects of this broken world.

He goes on in the next two verses to acknowledge that when we truly understand that we have a far superior form of existence still to come, it causes us to groan, suddenly aware of the inferiority of the dwelling we find ourselves in now. Here is that peek into God's incredible design once again: Suffering is one of the clearest ways we gain this eternal perspective, whether it be a tragedy that jolts us from our comfortable life and illuminates the ills we once found easier to ignore, or a more tangible, physical pain that quite literally causes us to groan for the pain-free bodies we long to receive.

· ·

Suffering is one of the clearest ways we gain an eternal perspective.

· ·

In verse 4 we really see the crux of the deeper conflict come to life, as Paul says, "While we are still in this tent, we groan, being bur-dened—*not that we would be unclothed, but that we would be further clothed, so that what is mortal may be swallowed up by life"* (emphasis added). Paul holds space in the unique tension between two seemingly contradictory ideas here, bringing much-needed nuance to what could otherwise cause despair. He doesn't say, "So the sooner we can throw off this tent, the better, because this miserable existence is just an inferior pit stop on our way to eternity." Instead, he intentionally points out that our mentality is not to be one of hating the human existence or seeking to escape it—"not that we would be unclothed"—but rather, "that we would be *further* clothed, so that what is mortal may be swallowed up by life" (emphasis added). Paul isn't calling us to self-hatred or promoting suicidal fantasies; he's pointing to a deeper, more complex view of eternity, where we will find perfect completion.

Remember that a tent wouldn't necessarily have called to mind pictures of a miserable existence that bears no resemblance to home for the Corinthians, an insight that helps illuminate Paul's perspective more clearly here. There is still life to be experienced in the tent, and there is purpose for our time here. We can even be grateful for the way the tent has sheltered us well, and yet still be ever mindful of the reality that something better awaits us at home.

Paul isn't presenting eternity in heaven as the opposite of everything about our life here, but as the eventual perfection of it. A thread of continuity runs through Paul's perspective, because the human soul runs an unbroken continuum from the moment of our creation to the boundless depths of eternity. That is why he is careful to teach this idea of our completion in the perfection of eternity. He doesn't teach about heaven as a complete erasure of all that we are, only to be replaced with something better—as that would at best render meaningless every moment of our human life, and at worst make our very existence an outright subversion of God's plan for us and a barrier to His kingdom coming.

As the passage continues in verses 5 and 6, the picture of this seemingly precarious balance gets clearer:

> He who has prepared us for this very thing is God, who has given us the Spirit as a guarantee. So we are always of good courage. We know that while we are at home in the body we are away from the Lord.

Here's a hidden nugget I really want to make sure we don't miss here, the truth of an intentional design from a perfect and faithful Creator echoed once again. He has "prepared us," Paul says. Not only has He perfectly prepared us, but He's also given us His Spirit as full assurance of His promise to one day deliver our perfect completion, and also as undeniable proof that He is working in us even now.

When we understand this carefully balanced perspective that Paul fleshes out for us in the first seven verses, we can read the final line of the passage not from a place of cynicism or depression, but with that same perspective of our completion in mind. "Yes, we are of good courage, and we would rather be away from the body and at home with the Lord" (verse 8).

Finding Balance

Paul calls this church of believers to be wary of getting too comfortably situated in this earthly tent, forgetting about the palace that awaits them (and us). And yet, we miss the mark if we simply read this as a call to abandon the world and eschew our time here as meaningless. Being eternity-minded does not require us to hate the world or deny the beauty we find in this life, but rather to see our joys as a mere preview of so much that is better and yet to come, and to see our suffering as temporary afflictions that will no longer remain when His perfect work in us comes to completion.

Finding such balance is usually difficult. In fact, this letter to the Corinthians isn't the only place we see Paul wrestling with how to stand in the tension. In his letter to the Philippians, written entirely from the confines of imprisonment, we find an epistle saturated with themes of suffering. Yet this rather short letter (Philippians is only four chapters long) contains more than ten combined uses of the noun "joy" (*chara* in Greek) and the verb "rejoice" (*chairō*). We're going to discuss that seemingly contradictory set of ideas in a later chapter, but for now I want to take a quick peek at something Paul says in chapter 1 of this epistle.

> To me to live is Christ, and to die is gain. If I am to live in the flesh, that means fruitful labor for me. Yet which I shall choose I cannot tell. I am hard pressed between the two. My desire is to depart and be with Christ, for that is far better. But to remain in the flesh is more necessary on your account. Convinced of this, I know that I will remain and continue with you all, for your progress and joy in the faith, so that in me you may have ample cause to glory in Christ Jesus, because of my coming to you again (verses 21-26).

In this passage we see Paul truly agonizing over how to balance the pull from two opposing directions. Remembering that Paul was writing this in chains, it's understandable that he seems even more anguished here than he does in the letter to the Corinthians. He is vulnerably admitting that his desire to be in heaven is far stronger than his desire to continue forward in this life, a sentiment I think anyone who has experienced prolonged suffering can relate to on a deeply personal level.

I am no exception. There was a point in my life where the years of consistent emotional trauma, as well as the relentless physical pain and disability, seemed like more than I could humanly bear. I found myself pleading a version of these verses in lament, begging God to just take me to heaven so I could leave this earthly pain behind. I was no longer standing in that tension, no longer trying to hold a difficult balance between the pull of these two sides. I had simply let go of one side entirely, letting the other completely pull me under.

If you find yourself reading these verses and thinking the weight of your burdens is simply too heavy to bear...if even a small part of you hears, "To die is gain," and wants to plead with God to take you from this world...*please reach out for help*. Yes, we have hope in Jesus, and yes, His grace is sufficient, but there are times when we need to seek out professional help to carry our burdens. This isn't a lack of faith; it takes wisdom to admit our own limitations and embrace the help of the people God calls to our aid. You wouldn't be holding this book in your hands today if I had not admitted both to myself and to those I love that I needed help to fight my way back to stand in that place of holy tension again.

Ultimately, Paul kept fighting for that balance, and he was able to find not only purpose in his sufferings, but joy as well. I think his willingness to embrace this tension between our present world and the hope of a perfect eternity played a vital role in being able to reach that joy. When we swing too far to one side and view this earthly life as meaningless, we give way to cynicism and depression and snuff out any flickers of gratitude or hope. Yet for most of us the greater danger is when we swing too far in the other direction and dedicate ourselves wholly to our lives here on earth. Where depression leaves us feeling constantly burdened by its weight, a mind that is consumed by the temporal will rarely feel the ache of what it has lost. It is as if we spend each of our days upgrading and redecorating our tent, blissfully unaware that we've chosen to remain in the wilderness rather than journey onward toward our glorious destination.

Seeing the Kingdom

In many ways, a life of comfort is the greatest potential stumbling block to a real and deepening faith. I firmly believe this is the reason Jesus said it would be easier for a camel to pass through the eye of a needle than for a rich man to enter the kingdom of heaven (Matthew 19:23-24). Many of the times I have heard this story taught, it was presented as though Jesus essentially tells the rich young ruler that he needs to sell everything he owns and give it to the poor, or he won't be saved. That never made sense to me, as Scripture is perfectly consistent in the teaching that salvation is by grace alone and never contingent on works (Ephesians 2:8-9; John 1:12; 5:24; Romans 6:23; 10:9). It would be an outright contradiction of that truth to have Jesus saying that this man's very salvation hinged on his own ability to execute a certain set of commands.

I believe part of the confusion here comes when we take the phrase "kingdom of God" and view it as referring solely to the place we go after we die. I get a very different perspective when I think of the Lord's prayer, when Jesus prays, "Your *kingdom* come, your will be done, *on earth as it is in heaven*" (Matthew 6:10, emphasis added). I think Jesus is speaking of entering the kingdom of heaven in Matthew 19:23-24 not as a reference to salvation and a literal rescue from hell, but rather in reference to this larger idea of the kingdom as it exists even now on this earth. I hear Him saying that a comfortable life of wealth and abundance is an enormous barrier to being able to take up our cross and follow wholly after Him. He's not saying that the wealthy can't be His disciples, but that ultimately it would be much more difficult for them to choose the cross of Christ over the trappings of this world.

That alluring draw toward the things of this world has always been strong, and for our current generation, there is certainly no exception. The demands on our time and attention are endless, and there's no shortage of distractions to numb our sense of eternity. We can so easily build our goals, our plans, our social network, our home, our acclaim, and our carefully crafted identity without ever feeling the damaging effects of our spiritual neglect. That is, until tragedy strikes or until pain cuts through the comfortable facade and focuses our vision so we can more clearly see the truth: These temporary things were never meant to satiate our hunger for heaven. Suffering increases the hunger so that we can no longer suppress it with empty distractions, forcing us to confront the pangs from deep within our gut.

Perhaps this is why Jesus consistently displayed a deep affinity for the poor, the sick, and the grieving. It is not simply that we see Him spending so much of His ministry surrounding Himself with the most marginalized and humbled segments of society—we can see this truth repeated all throughout His teachings as well.

Let's consider the beatitudes, for example. In Matthew 5–7 we find the famous Sermon on the Mount, a series of teachings Jesus delivered to His closest disciples very early in His ministry. In this passage He sets the stage for them, giving them the essential building blocks to understanding what the gospel is all about. The beatitudes are the opening to this entire message (5:2-12), where Jesus lists out nine categories of people He designates as "blessed."

Don't brush over this context: It's no coincidence that in a sermon where Jesus is highlighting for His disciples the core essentials that would serve as a foundation for their ministry, He chooses to give them this list as the foundation's cornerstone. The beatitudes give us a unique glimpse into the very heart of Christ. The nine types of people Jesus calls "blessed" are as follows:

1. the poor in spirit

2. those who mourn

3. the meek

4. those who hunger and thirst for righteousness

5. the merciful

6. the pure in heart

7. the peacemakers

8. those who are persecuted for righteousness' sake

9. those experiencing persecution on Jesus's account

Take a minute to go back through the labels on that list one by one, and place each into one of two categories. Category A is for character traits we could cultivate daily with our choices, behavior, and attitude. These would be similar to the fruits of the Spirit, for example (love, joy, peace, patience, kindness, goodness, faithfulness, gentleness, and self-control [Galatians 5:22-23]). Category B is for descriptions of difficult or painful circumstances we might experience but would rarely seek out or look to intentionally cultivate in our life. These are descriptors for people we would more commonly plan to minister to rather than people we would seek to become. Go ahead and mark each trait with an A or B now.

Did you catch that? Almost half of these "qualities" Jesus declares to His disciples as "blessed" are in fact *people* experiencing some form of pain and suffering in their lives. If Jesus is laying the groundwork for their ministry here, homing in on His most essential commands and teachings, does it seem odd that He would open the message with a list of qualities they seemingly cannot control? Why take time to intentionally designate these groups of the hurting as people so dear to His heart and so vital to His kingdom? While we ruminate on these questions for a moment, there's one other point I'd like us to consider.

The first item in this list, the very first thing Jesus wanted His disciples to understand about the gospel, was not simply, "Blessed are the poor in spirit," but also, "Theirs is the kingdom of heaven." Just like we saw in the story of the rich young ruler, Jesus is urgently pointing our attention to the very same truth. When we are the poorest in spirit, when suffering bears down heavy and grief robs us of everything we hold most dear, and when we find ourselves stripped bare of all that we used to live for and define ourselves by, *that* is when we are able to see the kingdom most clearly. In fact, the eighth category on this list is those who are facing persecution, and Jesus uses that same promise again—"Theirs is the kingdom of heaven."

Why would Jesus spend half of this list describing painful circumstances that are experienced, rather than positive character traits we can control with our daily choices? Because suffering matters. There is something so uniquely powerful about the experience of suffering that no other spiritual discipline can produce the same sort of shift in perspective. Suffering is the key to gaining an eternal view, to living not only as a people anchored firmly in the assurance of heavenly glory to come, but also as fully endowed citizens of the kingdom of heaven here and now on this earth.

Let's return to 2 Corinthians to see one final piece of perspective from Paul.

> We do not lose heart. Though our outer self is wasting away, our inner self is being renewed day by day. For this light momentary affliction is preparing for us an eternal weight of glory beyond all comparison, as we look not to the things that are seen but to the things that are unseen.

For the things that are seen are transient, but the things
that are unseen are eternal (4:16-18).

We do not lose heart, because we know that this body is temporary, but our soul is eternal. We are not simply to bide our time here
waiting for God to destroy all this and replace it with something else
entirely; rather, we are to remember that as our outer shell is wast-
ing away, our eternal soul is being renewed day by day. Not only can
we know that the suffering of this life is momentary in light of eternity; we can also know that none of our pain is ever wasted. This
life and its sorrows aren't meaningless, because He is using all of it
to prepare us for "an eternal weight of glory beyond all comparison."
Rather than trying to escape our suffering, we can embrace our pain
as the key to unlocking an eternal perspective, helping us clearly dis-
cern between the transient distractions and the treasure that is worth
storing up in heaven.

Paul manages to take our two seemingly conflicting ideas and
bring them together in harmony, providing that perfect balance we
keep wrestling to hold on to. These three small verses embody a vast
theology of great depth that throws off the comfort of simplistic
extremes and trite, bumper-sticker answers, teaching us to choose
instead to meet with God inside the holy tension of it all.

It would seem far easier for some of us to say, "Everything in this
life is meaningless; only heaven matters." For others, we feel most
at ease when we take the limited time we have in this life and dedicate ourselves wholly to making the most of it. Yet, the truths of this
chapter are much like one of those optical-illusion picture books so
many of us had as children: If we focus too much on just one small
part of the page, the real picture never comes into view. It's only
when we let go of our misdirected focus, when we step back to hold
the whole page in patient surrender, that somehow the illusion is

separated out and the hidden beauty finally comes into view. The kingdom of God can only be seen clearly with that same patient surrender, that same willingness to embrace the discomfort of releasing the illusion of simple answers, all to see the deeper beauty that's hidden from our earthly view.

So how can we intentionally seek this eternal perspective each day? When life is comfortable, ask God where you can find more of that eternal view. Begin by recognizing and lamenting the suffering of others and intentionally seek out community with the marginalized and oppressed. If your load is light, see that as a position of responsibility to help shoulder the burden of others. When there are good things in your life, recognize them as a small taste of the far greater glory yet to come. Practice gratitude without ever losing the hunger for more than this life can fill.

When you experience pain, let it increase your longing for the perfect and pain-free body He has faithfully promised you in eternity. When there is death and loss, remind yourself that while our temporary bodies will die, our souls are eternal and can never be snatched from His hand. When there is inadequacy, hold firm to the promise that He who began a good work in you will be faithful to bring it to completion (Philippians 1:6).

Most importantly, remember that the place of perfect balance will also be the place of strongest tension. Perhaps this is why Paul writes in Romans that we are to "be transformed by the renewal of [our] mind" (Romans 12:2). These are not simplistic truths we can easily master and then file away as we move on to something new; instead, they present us with a consistent, ongoing battle between the pull of two sides. It is only as we seek that continued renewal of our minds, day after day, again and again, that we can present ourselves to be constantly realigned and rebalanced once more.

God, in His infinite and perfect wisdom, has created you for the life you've been given, and He has purpose for each breath of your lungs and beat of your heart. Nothing about your time on this earth is meaningless, so take heart: He is using all of it to prepare you for a glory beyond anything you can imagine. The things of earth will one day grow strangely dim, and you will watch Paul's words unfold before you as "what is mortal [is] swallowed up by life" (2 Corinthians 5:4). I know that He who began a good work in you will be faithful to bring it to completion. Cling tightly to this promise.

Chapter 4

Holy Intimacy

Grief knits two hearts in closer bonds than happiness ever can;
and common sufferings are far stronger links than common joys.

Alphonse de Lamartine[1]

When I was four years old, my mother brought me to my very first ballet class. It was love at first plié. I drifted in and out of a number of extracurricular activities through the years, but dance was a constant, and my passion only grew. By junior high I had been a vocal part of getting dance added to the arts program of my Christian school, and over the years I had not only become the department's most recognizable dancer, but eventually its first ever student teacher as well. I was fully prepared to pursue dance professionally, with the goal of opening my own studio to teach once I had aged out of a company. Dance wasn't just a hobby or mode of self-expression—it had become a calling.

Something else had happened when I was a child, though, an event so small that it had passed without anyone even noticing. It is sometimes hard to reconcile that the most pivotal moment of my life, an event that irreparably changed so much of who I am, is something I'll never be able to remember. I'll never know for sure when that moment occurred, only that I was about 16 years old when its effects first became visible.

It began with episodes we called "breathing attacks." One minute I would be perfectly fine; the next I would quite suddenly be desperate for air, unable to draw more than shallow, painful breaths. My doctor at the time couldn't find a clear diagnosis, but she set me up with an emergency inhaler and the go-ahead to keep dancing. Then came bouts of random dizziness and even fainting. I grew inexplicably clumsy, suffering a string of repeated dance injuries from broken toes to sprained ankles, and eventually a series of torn ligaments in my dominant leg.

By my senior year of high school, I was plagued with nearly constant fatigue. I could sleep 10 to 12 hours a night and still find it impossible to get dressed each morning. By this point, the injuries could no longer be explained by dance alone. I found myself covered in bruises without any memory of what might have caused them; my joints would give out seemingly without cause; and I was in nearly constant chronic pain that didn't seem to have a source. I was having cognitive problems, as well, and I was finding it harder and harder to remember choreography. My grades at school had all plummeted.

I will never forget the day when, at 18 years old, I sat in front of the dance department students, and the room filled with tears and cries of disbelief as I announced that I would no longer be dancing in any capacity. I would remain to serve as a teaching assistant for our final months, but I had performed my last solo, led my last competition team, and withdrawn from my more serious dance classes outside of school as well. I was sure this was the defining moment of my faith, that I would always look back on this as the hardest day of my life: when I was asked to give up my identity and surrender without question to God's greater plan.

I was determined to prove that this had not shaken my walk with Christ. I was going to will myself to simply choose joy. I resolved to find the lesson God was teaching me in this and focus only on the positives. I would find new passions and new callings, and I would prove that God had a clear plan for taking dance from me. Most of all, I was certain of one thing: God would never take all this away if He wasn't going to replace it with something so much more fulfilling. I truly believed that God had made me a dancer so that He could send this mystery illness into my life, knowing that everyone who saw my positive attitude and unbreakable faith would see His faithfulness on full display when a bigger and better future would finally unfold.

That sweet 18-year-old girl, waiting confidently in faith for God to show up in power on the other side of her pain? She was so certain, and yet so wholly naive. If only she could somehow see what was still to come. There would be epilepsy, memory loss, arthritis, fibromyalgia, irreversible heart damage, kidney damage, neurological problems, a tremor, and watching a once capable mind devolve into aphasia and loss of even basic functions. Chronic fatigue would only worsen through the years until I was effectively bedridden much of the time. There would be two separate bouts of lymphoma, and treatments for cancer would be difficult and draining. There would be the seven painful miscarriages and two difficult and harrowing pregnancies with life-threatening complications. There would be panic attacks, anxiety, and the depression that comes from feeling trapped in a body that would rob me of so many choices. Worse, there would be over a decade's worth of doctors who wouldn't be able to find a definitive explanation. Some would offer conflicting guesses and lists of constantly changing diagnoses; others would think I was perhaps exaggerating or seeking attention; and some would even suggest my symptoms could be the physical manifestations of a purely psychological illness.

After 14 long years of battling this mystery beast that had stolen so much of my life, the diagnosis would finally come with a whimper, not a bang. I had Lyme disease. The invisible event that had taken place all those years ago? It was a simple tick bite, one I never noticed or even knew to look for in the first place. Yet it irreparably affected every facet of my life from that day forward.

Lyme disease begins as a basic bacterial infection, so it could have been treated with a few weeks of oral antibiotics if we had only known that the bite had occurred. Instead, the bacteria had been left to multiply and wage war on my body for 14 years straight, eventually burrowing deep into the tissue of my organs to make itself harder to detect or eradicate. Even though a diagnosis had finally come, it would not bring the relief I'd always dreamed it would. Late-stage Lyme is often impossible to cure, and even if we could manage to kill the Lyme and the viral coinfections, I would still be left with permanent damage to parts of my brain, heart, and other vital organs.

That 18-year-old me was completely confident in her claims that God would show up in power on the other side of this pain and that the answers to make sense of it all were just around the bend. I had charged onward only to discover more questions around those bends, and no matter how far I kept walking forward in faith, the "other side" of my pain never appeared over the horizon.

That 18-year-old me had turned into 21-year-old me, and then 25, and then 30. No matter how many inspirational reminders I put up, no matter how many times I told myself to "just choose joy," and no matter how fervently I professed that happiness was a choice, I was still human, and the cracks in my facade grew more and more visible over time.

I tried to keep putting on a brave face. I lived for the times people would tell me I was "inspirational," or how encouraged they were to see me keep up that bubbly personality despite such horrible circumstances. Privately, though, I felt a deeply cutting shame at the fear, doubt, sadness, and even anger growing underneath my carefully maintained image. I felt more and more distant from God, and so I threw myself even more aggressively into proclaiming His goodness and the strength of my faith.

Sometimes I wonder if I was secretly trying to manipulate God, perhaps believing that if I showed myself to be a deserving person of faith, He would have no choice but to show up and prove His goodness to those who were watching. I think that, more often than not, I was simply trying to fake it until He could make it, believing that if I just kept trying to have a doubtless faith, He would inevitably transform my heart and make it true. I had developed a theology in which it was essential to downplay or even outright ignore my suffering in order to grow closer to Christ. Faith, to me, was being able to exuberantly embrace my circumstances without any lament or complaint. It wasn't good enough to survive; I should appear to do it effortlessly. Faith was a weight lifter casually tossing an anvil on his shoulder and saying with a smirk, "Oh, this little thing?"— as if a single grunt, grimace, or bead of sweat might betray his inner weakness after all.

The day I found myself on the bathroom floor was the day I finally let go of—or rather, was *forced* to let go of—my misplaced notions of faith. The flowery affirmations of that 18-year-old girl had been replaced by guttural howls of lament. There was no bubbly facade, just globs of smeared mascara across hot, red cheeks. I had no fight left in me, no strength to push down my grief and seek a more cheerful heart. I lay on that bathroom floor with the toilet paper roll hanging above me as a white flag of surrender. It was there that the warrior faith I had clung to all those years suffered a final, fatal blow, a wound that would literally bleed out of me over the coming weeks, staining my favorite pair of pajamas.

That night, on that floor, I felt the presence of Jesus more vividly than I had ever experienced before. I wasn't miraculously calmed—in fact, quite the opposite: I sobbed and heaved and even raged. Yet, somehow, I felt a deeper connection to Christ than in any previous years of supposedly stalwart faith. I didn't understand it. I just knew that Jesus had drawn near right there on that linoleum. I had spent so many years trying to push past my pain and chase after Christ alone, but there He was meeting me inside my pain.

Meet a Sorrowful Jesus

Jesus was in the very last place I would have looked for Him. He met me in my lament, in my sorrow, in my questions, in my fear, in my troubled spirit. But how could that be? Fear and faith are usually presented as opposite ends of a spectrum. We are taught that we can't embrace fear and be a person of true faith. And isn't a troubled spirit a sign that we are not grounded enough in Scripture, or that our spiritual transformation as a Christian is somehow lacking?

The thing is, Jesus had a bathroom floor story too—or, more accurately, a garden floor story. In the midst of the dramatic plot elements of the Last Supper, the Crucifixion, the death of Jesus, and a triumphant victory over the grave, three of the four Gospel writers carved out an intentional space for this small story right in the heart of it all. It's where we see Jesus head into the garden of Gethsemane to pray.

Most people have a passing familiarity with this scene insofar as they know that Jesus prays in the garden, and they might even remember Sunday-school stories of His sleepy disciples who can't seem to stay awake for their friend. For the most part, though, the story we recall is that Jesus pauses in the garden to pray, saying He's fully surrendered to God's will and ready for what He knows is about to come, and then the soldiers show up, and the plot moves along to the Crucifixion. Yet, there is much more to be found in examining the three accounts of this seemingly small story, and there is a question we should keep in mind as we continue: Why was it so essential to include the story of Gethsemane at all?

Jesus's time in the garden is recorded in Matthew 26:36-46, Mark 14:32-42, and Luke 22:39-46. Like most accounts that show up in multiple Gospels, the story itself is consistent, but the details the writers focus on can vary. I want to look at a theme that is consistent throughout the accounts.

- "He began to be sorrowful and troubled. Then he said to them, 'My soul is very sorrowful, even to death'" (Matthew 26:37-38).

- "[He] began to be greatly distressed and troubled. And he said to them, 'My soul is very sorrowful, even to death. Remain here and watch'" (Mark 14:33-34).

Sorrowful. Distressed. Troubled. The perfect and sinless Savior of the world is described with words we so often consider markers of a lack of true faith. How could His spirit be troubled when He knew exactly what was going to unfold, that He would rise on the third day to conquer sin and death? How could He be distressed or sorrowful? Shouldn't an attitude of faithful submission to the Father mean refusing to get bogged down in negative feelings? Most importantly, how is any of this possible in Jesus, a sinless example of perfection?

I struggled with this last question for some time, especially when I read on to look at the prayer itself.

- "Going a little farther he fell on his face and prayed, saying, 'My Father, if it be possible, let this cup pass from me; nevertheless, not as I will, but as you will'" (Matthew 26:39).

- "Going a little farther, he fell on the ground and prayed that, if it were possible, the hour might pass from him. And he said, 'Abba, Father, all things are possible for you. Remove this cup from me. Yet not what I will, but what you will'" (Mark 14:35-36).

- "He withdrew from them about a stone's throw, and knelt down and prayed, saying, 'Father, if you are willing, remove this cup from me. Nevertheless, not my will, but yours, be done'" (Luke 22:41-42).

I've heard the garden prayer so often summarized as, "Not my will, but yours, be done," yet that's only a small part of what was prayed, and it leaves out the larger context. A sorrowful Jesus with a deeply troubled spirit comes to the garden so distressed that He literally falls to the ground pleading. This isn't a picture of brave and casual detachment, nor do we see a doubtless prayer, as though Jesus were saying, "Sure, this will be difficult, but I'm totally unfazed by it all because of My faith in You, Lord." This is something so much more human. It's just as much a picture of struggle, fear, and distress as one of obedient submission.

And lest we think this is just a small, passing phrase, where Jesus briefly admits His humanity for our sake and then pulls Himself together going forward, the continuing story shows us something very different. Jesus prays and pleads, but then He checks on His disciples, who were supposed to be praying and supporting Him. When He finds them asleep, He wakes them up and urges them to be with Him in this, only to begin the very same pleading prayer again. The whole cycle repeats once more, and so three separate times we see Jesus anxiously pleading for some other way out or for the strength to bear what must be done in the end.

As I studied these passages, I continued to find myself overwhelmed with questions. How could a perfect and sinless Savior be portrayed as anything less than a brave paragon of warrior-like faith? How could He possibly beg for a way out and still be seen as obediently submitting to God's will? Reading further in Luke's account only amplified these questions for me, because right after Jesus begs for the cup to be removed from Him, we see this:

> There appeared to him an angel from heaven, strengthening him. And being in agony he prayed more earnestly; and his sweat became like great drops of blood falling down to the ground (Luke 22:43-44).

Now we have a distressed Jesus weeping and pleading on the ground, begging God to spare Him from this, and instead of God being more distant from this apparent lack of faith, God sends an angel from heaven to minister to Jesus as He prays. The verse even says that the angel strengthens Him. So, surely, He is then overcome with the peace of God and strengthened by a warrior-like faith to run headfirst into His fate with pure, unmitigated joy, right? Surely He leaps right up from that ground, runs straight to those disciples, and joyfully reminds them to take heart, because He would be coming back soon, and God's power would be on full display. But no. That's not at all what happens.

The angel arrives, strengthening Him, and the very next sentence we read says, "*Being in agony he prayed more earnestly*; and his sweat became like great drops of blood falling down to the ground" (verse 44, emphasis added). The angel strengthening Him doesn't cause Him to rise up out of the depths of suffering—it strengthens Him to go deeper inside it. Distress becomes outright agony, tears of sorrow become beads of blood, and His pleading prayers don't end, but continue on more earnestly than before.

Let's return to our earlier question: Why was it essential to include this Gethsemane story in the Gospel accounts? What possible benefit could there be in showing the Savior of the world as weak, distressed, agonized, and so very human?

Within the story, Jesus actually tries three different times to bring His closest disciples into this scene, waking them from their sleep and calling them to experience this agonizing display of pain alongside Him. But why? Why would He want them to see Him as anything less than bravely leading them onward, without any fear or trepidation?

An Invitation from Christ

I think these repeated invitations to the disciples are the very same invitation that the story is meant to offer us today: "Come and know Me more intimately in suffering." We may believe that it's not true obedience unless it's performed with a cheerful and unquestioning attitude, and without any significant wrestling or temptation to disobey. We may think that a trial is not faithfully endured if we express doubts, ask the Lord to take it from us, or fail to keep up a positive and encouraging demeanor through it all. Yet none of these ideas are consistent with the Jesus we see in the garden. This story illustrates a truth we miss in a lot of our broken theologies of suffering: By downplaying our personal pain and pretending we are unaffected by our trials, we miss the opportunity to connect with Jesus and know Him more intimately.

The apostle Paul was able to flesh out this idea beautifully in his letter to the Philippians.

The angel
strengthening
Him doesn't
cause Him
to rise up out
of the depths
of suffering—it
strengthens
Him to go
deeper inside it.

I count everything as loss because of the surpassing worth of knowing Christ Jesus my Lord. For his sake I have suffered the loss of all things and count them as rubbish, in order that I may gain Christ and be found in him, not having a righteousness of my own that comes from the law, but that which comes through faith in Christ, the righteousness from God that depends on faith—*that I may know him and the power of his resurrection, and may share his sufferings, becoming like him in his death* (3:8-10, emphasis added).

Let's also take a quick peek at that last verse in a different translation. This version gives Paul's words a different dimension, which helped me better grasp the passion at the core of his message:

I want to know Christ—yes, to know the power of his resurrection and participation in his sufferings, becoming like him in his death (Philippians 3:10 NIV).

"I want to know Christ" is the thesis statement of this entire passage. Paul's singular goal here is to push us toward knowing Jesus, and knowing Him more intimately. With that in mind, we can go back to the beginning of our passage to see what Paul is teaching us. In verse 8, Paul says that he counts everything as worthless, because the worth of knowing Jesus is that much better than anything else in this world. He reframes his sentiment again even more personally, saying that he himself has suffered the loss of all things so that he may gain Christ.

It would be easy to read this verse as saying there are no material possessions you could ever own that would be as good as knowing Jesus, but that's not all Paul is getting at here. This becomes clearer in the next verse.

In verse 8, the goal is to "gain Christ." That phrase leads directly into verse 9, where Paul continues, "And be found in him, not having a righteousness of my own that comes from the law, but that which comes through faith in Christ." Those things Paul asks us to count as loss in order to know Christ aren't just material possessions or earthly enjoyments. He's also speaking of our striving, our good works, and those perfected facades.

I spent so many years performatively shrugging and quipping, "Count it all loss!" whenever people asked about something my illness had taken from me, all the while unaware that it was also my very determination to keep soldiering on that I was being asked to lay down. What I was calling my "faith in Christ" was actually "a righteousness of my own that comes from the law," and I was gripping it far too tightly to surrender.

Paul is calling us here to embrace the loss of even some of our most fervently held beliefs and ideas as a key to knowing Jesus. He's calling us to embrace the loss of our confidence, the loss of our ability to hold it all together, the loss of the appearance of righteousness, the loss of having all the answers, the loss of feeling in control of our own life, the loss of our pedestal before others who have looked up to us.

To see this idea backed up more clearly, read through Philippians 3:4-6, the verses preceding our passage. They share what's essentially a laundry list of evidence of Paul's personal "righteousness," culminating in his declaration that "whatever gain I had, I counted as loss for the sake of Christ" (verse 7). We were never called to try harder to keep up these appearances of bravery; we were told to let go and count it all as loss.

> We were never called to try harder to keep up these appearances of bravery; we were told to let go and count it all as loss.

It's after all these urgings toward loss that we find ourselves back at verse 10 and the reason for it all: "I want to know Christ" (NIV). But remember, the verse doesn't end there.

> I want to know Christ—yes, to know the power of his resurrection and *participation in his sufferings*, becoming like him in his death (Philippians 3:10 NIV, emphasis added).

Paul takes knowing Jesus and the power of His resurrection and directly connects this with an invitation to participate in His sufferings. The first time I read that phrase it took my breath away—"participation in his sufferings" (NIV). Peter actually echoes this same sentiment in the letter we looked at in chapter 2. Remember what we read? "Beloved, do not be surprised at the fiery trial when it comes upon you to test you, as though something strange were happening to you" (1 Peter 4:12). In the very next verse, he adds, "But rejoice insofar as you *share Christ's sufferings*" (verse 13, emphasis added).

We have two different letters from two different authors, but both contain this teaching of suffering as a shared experience with Christ. Both writers reject a view of suffering as an obstacle distancing us from Jesus, choosing instead to elevate suffering as a sacred bond through which we commune directly with our Savior.

Jesus experienced anguish, fear, and sorrow in the garden, and instead of glossing over the realities of His suffering to put on a brave show of faith, He invited His disciples to connect with Him more deeply by witnessing and even participating in His suffering. Now Paul and Peter both call us to that same invitation: to know Christ more by communing with Him inside our own pain.

When I lay pleading on that linoleum floor, I was inexplicably connected to Christ pleading on the ground of Gethsemane. Each time I wept in grief as I lost another child, I was tethered to Jesus weeping in grief at His friend Lazarus's death (John 11:33-35). When my body was overcome with seemingly unbearable physical pain, I was joined in sacred bond with my Savior in the pain of crucifixion. The more I learned to let go of my brave facade and count it as loss, the more I could press deeply into knowing Christ more fully through participation in His sufferings.

This sacred intimacy holds more than our intertwined suffering though. "As we share abundantly in Christ's sufferings, so through Christ we share abundantly in comfort too" (2 Corinthians 1:5). We serve a God who willingly took on flesh and experienced the fullness of the pain, grief, and struggle found in the human existence. It is because of Christ's earthly suffering that we serve a God uniquely equipped to comfort us in our own pain and loss. I can't help but think of the gods in both classical Greek and Roman mythologies, deities who so often ignore or even revel in the suffering of humans down below. What a stark contrast Paul offers when he shares about our God, who doesn't comfort out of pity or try to manipulate humans for personal gain, but rather deeply understands our pain because He willingly walked among us and experienced it firsthand.

Too often we reduce the significance of the life of Christ to "He came to die for our salvation." Yet if the sole purpose of God's incarnation was to be killed as a sacrifice for our sins, He could just as easily have allowed Herod's soldiers to kill the infant Christ and accomplished the same end. We see in the Christmas story, though, that Jesus is very intentionally spared when an angel comes to Joseph and specifically directs the holy family to flee (Matthew 2:13), which serves as pretty solid evidence that Christ's continued life on this earth had more purpose than His death alone. Just as the goal of salvation is to end the divide sin has placed between our souls and our Creator, the suffering He willingly experienced throughout His time on this earth connects us more closely with Him as well.

The gospel offers a powerful message of a God who so relentlessly pursues our heart that He would not only choose to die for us, but to live for us as well. The Bible contains glimpses into His life while on this earth, but try to imagine the volume of experiences that happen in more than three decades of life. Picture every bruise, every illness, every scraped knee, every headache. Picture every tear, every loss, and every heartbreak. Picture every moment of feeling misunderstood, lonely, anxious, falsely attacked, bullied, undervalued, or misused. Every moment of human suffering that Christ willingly lived and endured was in pursuit of *you*, a chance not only to know you more intimately and draw you closer to Himself, but also to be equipped to comfort you perfectly in your own pain.

Fully Honest

This is the single most important reason to confront and root out prosperity-gospel thinking in our theologies: When our faith becomes marked by triumphalism and false positivity, we miss the intimacy with Christ that our pain makes uniquely possible. It is impossible to press deeper into the heart of Jesus or to participate in His sufferings if we are either looking for ways to avoid our pain or simply refusing to acknowledge it affects us. It's as if suffering is a magnet designed to pull us toward Christ, but prosperity-gospel theology reverses the polarity so that our suffering only creates greater distance from Him instead.

A painful illustration of this truth played out over a number of years in my marriage. The numerous miscarriages weighed heavily on me, and my grief was all-consuming, and yet I didn't share myself wholly with my husband and bore much of the pain privately. I believed it would better preserve our relationship if I could spare him from having to help carry me, and I was worried that he couldn't possibly love me as much if he saw me as too broken or too changed from the woman he first fell in love with. But walling off such an enormous part of my heart could never draw us together more intimately, and the invisible divide it created started to widen more with time. I began to resent Bobby deeply for not grieving as much as I did, assuming that he didn't love our children as much as I had. Despite the fact that I had hidden much of my pain away, I felt bitter that he didn't somehow see it anyway and shoulder part of my load. We had both lost these children, and yet we were each grieving separately. What could have been a deeply intimate experience where we shouldered each other's pain and comforted each other in a way that is only possible when two people know the same loss instead became a wedge between us, pushing us into our own separate worlds and growing deep resentments that took us years to begin untangling.

I'm able to look back now and see just how much I made this same mistake in my relationship with Christ. The false positivity I was so sure He wanted of me only widened the divide and led me to secretly question His love for me. The more I attempted to carry my own pain and show Him just how strong I could be, the more removed I became from His strength and the chance to experience Him shouldering my burdens. When my poor theology of suffering ultimately led to doubts, frustrations, and even anger at God, I tried to hide my true feelings from Him even more—which only widened the divide further. As is true in a marriage, the only chance I had to reverse this

cycle and relearn how to connect more intimately was to communicate the whole truth with downright painful honesty.

Bobby and I couldn't begin to reverse the damage done by the
years of walling off my grief until I was able to admit to him my bitterness and resentment, giving him the first real chance to respond.
In the same way, by trying to hide my feelings from God, I wasn't
giving Him a chance to speak to my resentments, disappointments,
bitterness, and doubts. Much like I had worried that my true brokenness would dampen Bobby's love for me, I feared God wouldn't
love me as much if I admitted just how human I really was. That
night on the bathroom floor, when all the pretense disappeared
and I simply didn't have the strength to pretend any longer, I was
fully honest with God for the first time in many years. I had always
assumed that owning my pain and admitting my doubts would
be the beginning of the end for my relationship with Him, but it
proved to be the turning point that opened up a level of intimacy I
had never even imagined possible.

That night, I repeated over and over, "I don't understand, God.
I just don't understand." As my walls came down and my honesty
grew, my lament became more desperate. I cried out, "How could
You do this to me, God? Have You just abandoned me? Do You
even care?" Eighteen-year-old me would have been horrified by
such a prayer, certain that this was blasphemy and likely to bring on
God's punishment and wrath. But that lament was a sacred thread,
drawn across time and connecting me directly to Christ on the cross:
"About the ninth hour Jesus cried out with a loud voice, saying, 'Eli,
Eli, lema sabachthani?' that is, '*My God, my God, why have you forsaken me?*'" (Matthew 27:46, emphasis added).

Just as Christ's anguished garden prayers obliterate the idea that
God requires a brave and unencumbered facade, His cry on the
cross creates space for honest, powerful lament. The desperate words

I feared would create a wedge between me and my Savior were but an echo of His own cries two thousand years earlier. This sacred thread doesn't end there though. The same lament that connected me from that cold linoleum floor to Christ in His crucifixion also runs back even further in connection to King David as well.

> My God, my God, why have you forsaken me? Why are you so far from saving me, from the words of my groaning? (Psalm 22:1).

What a powerful example of the connective tissue of suffering: David's broken cry sent heavenward, only to return to earth about a thousand years later, spoken by God in human form.

When Bobby and I went to a counselor to work through our grief divide, we were taught a common technique called reflective listening. In essence, we learned that the best way to communicate to someone that they are heard, and that the feelings they are expressing are important, is to repeat back their words to them before any sort of response. How incredible to see El Shama[2], "the God who hears," repeat back David's words of lament, giving them new depth as He cries out from the cross.

Seeing God connect to David in suffering makes the psalms about His comfort that much more meaningful.

- "The LORD is near to the brokenhearted and saves the crushed in spirit" (Psalm 34:18).
- "He heals the brokenhearted and binds up their wounds" (Psalm 147:3).

The Lord drew near to me on that bathroom floor, just as He drew near to David, and to the apostle Paul, and to all who bring their broken hearts and honest laments to Him. The God of the universe took on human form and bore all the suffering of the human experience so He could draw you into deeper intimacy with Himself.

Friend, don't be afraid to lean into your pain. Don't believe the lies that your brokenness will somehow be too much for God to love. Don't be deceived into glossing over your suffering with a cheerful smile or prosperity-gospel platitudes. Jesus isn't waiting on the other side of your pain, ready to show up in power after you've proven you are worthy—He's right there in the midst of it, longing to bind up your wounds and share in the suffering together. Bring Him your fears, your doubts, your pain, and your grief. Come exactly as you are, without any pretense. No matter how irreverent that honesty may feel, offering yourself more wholly to God without any walls or reservations is the first step to the most holy intimacy. "Draw near to God, and he will draw near to you" (James 4:8). Find your bathroom floor, your prison cell, your Gethsemane ground. Just show up, and I promise: He will meet you there.

Chapter 5

Personal Training

*I hoped faith would be an epidural for pain. Turns out to be
a midwife who says, "Push. I'm here. Sometimes it hurts."*

BRENÉ BROWN[1]

Growing up, my family attended a pretty mainstream, conservative Baptist church. Sunday mornings were spent both in Sunday-school classes and in "big church." Sunday nights were spent in rehearsals for the children's choirs while the parents attended the evening service. Wednesday nights were the parents' turns for choir rehearsals while the kids went to either Boys' Brigade or Pioneer Girls, the church alternatives to the secular Boy Scouts and Girl Scouts. We had calendars full of regular events through my parents' very close-knit Sunday-school class, which consisted of families with similarly aged children, who in turn became our closest friends as well. Many of these church families also attended the same local private Christian schools, so our lives were pretty consistently filled with either church functions or time spent with other members of our congregation.

Throughout the years, one undeviating warning carried throughout our spiritual formation: The secular world was full of influences looking to shake us from our faith and draw us into the clutching grasp of the greatest evil of all—moral relativism. The world, we were told, had given itself over to Satan's greatest lie, that we could all define our own truth and decide our own personal right and wrong. Moral relativism, we were told, was the single most dangerous obstacle to a faith that lasts a lifetime.

Much of our spiritual education was geared toward arming us with the tools we would need to withstand the attacks of this fallen world. We were regularly admonished to avoid the influences of secular movies, television shows, books, and most of all music, because the slippery slope could pull us downward in subtle increments, and we might not see our demise until it was too late. We learned that *tolerance* was an insidious word designed to convince us to open ourselves up and allow a foothold for moral relativism in the guise of love and understanding—a trap we would be well trained to identify and avoid. Bible memorization would arm us with all the verses we could need to prove the veracity of the Christian faith to questioners or to defeat any attempts to draw us into temptation. Participation in accountability groups would ensure that sin could be dealt with before it could pull us away from Jesus and thrust us into the waiting arms of the godless world. WWJD (What Would Jesus Do?) bracelets would not only remind us to avoid temptation, but they would also proclaim our Christian identity to the world and show them we were not ashamed of the gospel.

The goal of our time spent in both youth groups and Christian education was to turn out a generation of believers that could withstand all the trappings of this world. As well-trained Christians we would be marked by an unshakable certainty, entirely assured of what we believed and unplagued by questions or doubts. We would be bold and fearless, ready to unashamedly call out sin and false teaching wherever they were found. Our mission statement was perfectly encapsulated in a verse we all knew well: "In your hearts revere Christ as Lord. Always be prepared to give an answer to every-one" (1 Peter 3:15 NIV).

Take a second look at the verse reference above. Notice anything? We're back in 1 Peter, where we're told, "Beloved, do not be sur-prised at the fiery trial" (4:12). This is where we're reminded that we will "share Christ's sufferings" (verse 13), and we can "entrust [our] souls to a faithful Creator" while "suffer[ing] according to God's will" (verse 19). We know this is a letter written to the persecuted church in Asia Minor, specifically encouraging them to lean into their suf-fering and hold tightly to their faith in Christ.

So, are you surprised to find this verse (1 Peter 3:15 NIV) nestled right in the midst of that very same letter? I'll admit, I certainly was. This verse, and the corresponding teachings of my youth, didn't seem in any way compatible with my new understanding of suffer-ing and its vital role in the life of a believer.

We've just finished talking about Jesus as He was troubled and weeping in the garden and David lamenting of how forsaken he felt by God. How can any of that fit alongside a church striving to turn out a generation of Christians with unshakable confidence and absolute boldness, who have a perfect answer for every possi-ble question?

A Foundation of Suffering

Let's go back to fill in the details leading up to this verse from 1 Peter, to see if the context gives us a clearer understanding.

> Even if you should suffer for righteousness' sake, you will be blessed. Have no fear of them, nor be troubled, but in your hearts honor Christ the Lord as holy, always being prepared to make a defense to anyone who asks you for

a reason for the hope that is in you; yet do it with gentleness and respect (3:14-15).

Going back just one verse reveals something important right
away. The framework for this is once again the familiar motif of suffering. Peter's letter is undeviating in its theme of encouragement for
a church of believers who are bombarded by trials and persecution.

The communities in Asia Minor he writes to here bear seemingly little resemblance to the church of my childhood. For all the
warnings of the spiritual battles we would face, the members of my
church enjoyed a position of enormous privilege. We were located in
one of the most affluent cities in the heart of one of the most financially prosperous regions in the entire country. Our congregation was
predominantly white, able bodied, and upper or high middle-class.
Most importantly, we had the religious freedom to live out our faith
without any fear of real persecution. We had grown accustomed to
a certain level of comfort, and nowhere in our preparation for life in
the secular world had we been taught to expect anything different.

Peter's letter, though, is consistent in its directives to expect and
embrace suffering, and the church in Asia Minor would have had had
no difficulty understanding that this referred to their very tangible,
real-life struggles and not simply a spiritual battle of the mind. He
sets the stage in verse 14 of chapter 3 by referencing this same context of suffering before getting to the more famous exhortation in
the following verse. This is key to understanding what he's saying,
because although we are commonly taught "to give an answer to
everyone" (verse 15, NIV) in the context of Christian apologetics in
debates with nonbelievers, that's in no way an accurate reflection of
what Peter actually wrote. In fact, back in verse 8, Peter says, "All of
you, have unity of mind, sympathy, brotherly love, a tender heart,
and a humble mind."

So, Peter is not looking to depict a confident Christian student engaging in a spiritual battle of wits with an atheist college professor. This isn't the prequel to the movie *God's Not Dead*. Instead, we see these instructions in verse 8, calling us to have a tender heart, a spirit of sympathy and love, and—most importantly—a humble mind, meaning one that is consciously aware of its incomplete knowledge and its ability to make mistakes.

My childhood church emphasized total confidence in what we believe as the only armor against moral relativism and warned that adopting an attitude of "tolerance" would be the foothold that would let the enemy pull us under. Yet Peter gives a framework of listening with sympathy, a tender heart, and the humility to recognize that you could be just as wrong as the person sitting across from you. It is with the adoption of these attitudes in mind that Peter goes on in verse 15 to encourage these suffering believers with these words: "In your hearts honor Christ the Lord as holy, always being prepared *to make a defense* to anyone who asks you for a reason for the hope that is in you" (emphasis added).

I was struck by the wording in the ESV, "to make a defense," as contrasted with the phrasing I had originally learned from the NIV, "to give an answer." I immediately looked up the Greek to see if it offered any insight into which might be more accurate.

The word used here is *apologia* (ἀπολογία), which translates as a well-reasoned response or verbal speech in defense of something. It's especially helpful to understand that the Greek language is full of highly specialized words, often with very narrow and particular meanings, many of which often translate to a singular word in English. This particular word used here is responsive, meaning a defense is offered to a specific critique or charge.[2] It's not the word that would mean a testimony of something, *marturion* (μαρτύριον),[3] or the word that would be used for proof, *endeigma* (ἔνδειγμα),[4] or even a word that specifically means "indubitable evidence" or "that from which something is surely and plainly known," *tekmērion* (τεκμήριον).[5]

Reading all of this in context makes it clear that 1 Peter 3:15 was never meant to be a verse about preparing to debate a secular world in the name of the gospel. Instead, it's an admonition in the very same vein as "Do not be surprised at the fiery trial" (4:12). Peter warns these same believers to be prepared to make a defense because, just as our suffering is a certainty we should expect, so is the question that will inevitably come from those who witness that suffering: "What is the reason for the hope that is in you?" (see 3:15). Peter was never calling us to prepare for fiery online showdowns with unbelievers or to prove God's existence to skeptical scientists and atheist professors. He taught the same unwavering theme throughout his letter: Be prepared to suffer and aim to suffer well, because your suffering is a vital component of both the growth of your faith and your witness for the gospel.

Friend, we will always miss the mark when we attempt to separate a healthy theology of suffering from the gospel. A gospel that ignores human suffering, discounts its essential value, or claims to offer the key to avoiding it entirely is not the good news of Jesus. Despite the best of intentions from my church, the message I received in my youth lacked the depth and power of what Peter is ultimately preaching. No amount of Bible memorization or church participation could ever strengthen our faith and witness the way our suffering can. In fact, if we peek back to the very beginning of this letter, after Peter makes his opening introductions, these are some of his first thoughts:

> In this you rejoice, though now for a little while, if necessary, you have been grieved by various trials, so that the tested genuineness of your faith—more precious

than gold that perishes though it is tested by fire—may
be found to result in praise and glory and honor at the
revelation of Jesus Christ. Though you have not seen
him, you love him. Though you do not now see him,
you believe in him and rejoice with joy that is inexpress-
ible and filled with glory, obtaining the outcome of your
faith, the salvation of your souls (1 Peter 1:6-9).

Right from the beginning he identifies suffering as the foundation on which the rest of the teaching in his letter will stand.
He directly ties the sufferings of these embattled believers to the
strength and genuineness of their faith. It's a distinctly countercul-
tural idea—especially for the mainstream church—because it defies
any sensibilities of separating ourselves from a dangerous world.

So much of the spiritual upbringing I experienced was about creating fences between myself and the secular world until I could sufficiently grow my faith into one that would last a lifetime. What Peter
suggests here is quite the opposite, though—that the key to developing a strong faith isn't to nurture it in safety, but to welcome the
chance to develop it through adversity. Whereas the modern church
seeks to develop a more genuine belief in Christ inside the safety and
comfort of its walls, Peter paints a picture of a body whose faith is
flourishing as a direct result of their trials and persecution.

Peter's words become even more powerful when we consider
the line "though you have not seen him" (verse 8). Remember, he's
writing in a time when Jesus's death and resurrection are relatively
recent events, and there are still many believers walking the earth
who have had the benefit of witnessing Christ's miracles and ministry firsthand. Peter intentionally points out that although this is not
a church that received the benefits of firsthand witness, they have
a faith that's as genuine and powerful as if they had. If the goal of

discipleship is to mature simple belief into a meaningful faith that can last a lifetime, Peter is offering a picture of a church body that accomplished this with measurable success, and he points directly to their suffering as the key.

The Product of Suffering

This exact same sentiment is echoed by the apostle Paul in the book of Romans:

> Since we have been justified by faith, we have peace with God through our Lord Jesus Christ. Through him we have also obtained access by faith into this grace in which we stand, and we rejoice in hope of the glory of God. Not only that, but we rejoice in our sufferings, knowing that *suffering produces endurance,* and endurance produces character, and character produces hope, and hope does not put us to shame, because God's love has been poured into our hearts through the Holy Spirit who has been given to us (Romans 5:1-5, emphasis added).

Paul spends a majority of the book of Romans trying to work out the inherent tension between our salvation through Christ's grace and the role of our character in obedience to God's laws. He stands in yet another sacred place of seeming contradictions, embracing a salvation by grace alone that frees us from the bondage of the law, while holding equally to the truth that this salvation should be made evident through obedience to God. It's one of the most profound areas of tension in the gospel, and Paul wrestles with it faithfully in his relentless pursuit of knowing Christ more. He starts this passage in chapter 5 with a confirmation that our salvation ultimately comes by grace alone through faith in Jesus, a truth leading us to "rejoice in hope of the glory of God" (verse 2). It's the very core of the good

The key to
developing
a strong faith
isn't to nurture
it in safety,
but to welcome
the chance
to develop it
through adversity.

news: Through faith in Christ we receive a matchless grace that in turn produces our glorious hope.

But this isn't the only reason we should rejoice—Paul says we should also "rejoice in our sufferings" (verse 3). He then offers one of the most glowingly positive reviews for suffering I can imagine, explaining that our suffering will produce endurance, and that endurance will then in turn produce character, and that character will ultimately produce hope.

Did you catch that? Just as Christ's grace ultimately produces hope in us, our suffering does too. Paul stands squarely in the tension between our salvation by grace and our obedience to God's law and shows us the divine mystery of how these seemingly contradictory ideas find perfect harmony in Christ. It is by grace we receive the salvation that restores us to relationship with God, producing the hope of heaven and an eternity to dwell in His glory. But it is the development of our character that ultimately cements this hope, revealing glimpses of His glory while we're still here on earth.

A strikingly similar message can be found at the beginning of the book of James:

> Count it all joy, my brothers, when you meet trials of various kinds, for you know that the testing of your faith produces steadfastness. And let steadfastness have its full effect, that you may be perfect and complete, lacking in nothing (James 1:2-4).

Before we dive in further, I want to take a brief moment to offer a little context on the book of James, since you may find that some of the verses we'll examine have a very different tone and perspective than ones we've looked at from Paul.

James is viewed by many scholars as an example of Jewish

wisdom literature, in the same genre or style as the book of Proverbs. Wisdom, as seen in the Jewish tradition, isn't so much about knowledge or intellect, but about the type of character exhibited in godly living.[6] Robert F. Chaffin Jr. summarized it this way: "Their emphasis regarding wisdom was on the practical application of it, not on its theoretical or philosophical concepts."[7] Whereas modern readers most often think of wisdom as being internal, connected to our thinking processes or our understanding, "wisdom" in this context is more external, directly connected to our actions and our behavior toward others.

The word *wisdom* in this tradition could almost be interchangeable with the word *integrity*, as Jewish wisdom literature usually entails direct practical applications for areas of daily living. The book of James is no exception, being full of exhortations on how godly wisdom and faith in Christ should be evidenced in the life of a believer. James focuses heavily on the practical day-to-day implications of our new life in Christ, covering themes like how we should speak (1:26; 3:1-12; 4:11-12), how we should behave toward the poor (1:27; 2:1-17), and how we should avoid worldly temptation and behaviors (1:13-16; 4:1-10).

It is in this context that we find James echoing Paul's words that our suffering will produce in us endurance, which James refers to here as *steadfastness*. He implores his readers to "let steadfastness have its full effect" (1:4), once again affirming the idea that we should not seek to avoid suffering or downplay the very real pain we experience. In Romans, Paul says this endurance produces character, but James takes the concept even further, saying, "Let steadfastness have its full effect, that you may be perfect and complete, lacking in nothing" (verse 4). This is where understanding the context of James as wisdom teaching is key: Where the primary message of the Gospels is that redemption through Christ brings us back into relationship with God, the primary message of James is that this redemption can and should make us more like God. Like all Jewish wisdom teachers, James seeks to ensure that our *orthodoxy*—meaning what we believe—has a proper *orthopraxy* as well—meaning how we implement our beliefs and behave in response to them.

Of all the ways James could have opened this call to holiness, he begins with the foundation of a good theology of suffering. The theme here is consistent with the teachings we read from both Peter and Paul: Embrace your suffering, because it's the key to growing a genuine faith that will not only draw you closer to Jesus, but actually grow you to be more like Him as well. It should come as no surprise, then, that James also focuses heavily on themes of how we treat the suffering in our midst, since a wisdom text would speak primarily to the practical and outwardly visible fruits that becoming more like Christ should produce.

Remember when I shared about prosperity-gospel theology and the health-care debate? The book of James touches on this very issue in one of its most famous and challenging passages:

> Suppose a brother or a sister is without clothes and daily food. If one of you says to them, "Go in peace; keep warm and well fed," but does nothing about their physical needs, what good is it? In the same way, faith by itself, if it is not accompanied by action, is dead (2:15-17 NIV).

You've likely heard verse 17 before—or the wording from later in the passage: "Faith apart from works is dead" (verse 26). But did you know that this scripture comes from the specific context about how we treat the suffering in our midst? The verse is not a contradiction of the idea of salvation by grace alone; rather, it is another example of how James seeks to connect orthodoxy to orthopraxy, from wanting to know Christ more nearly to also embodying Him more clearly. The thread he uses to hold it all together is a healthy theology of suffering.

A Tapestry of Suffering

In this theology of suffering, our trials provide the key to better embodying Christlike wisdom, which in turn leads to a more genuine faith, one not only of belief but of practice. In the same way that Paul calls us to participate in Christ's suffering to know Him more intimately, James recognizes that that same participation will inevitably lead us to be more like Him as well. It is only logical that the best way to become more like a person we wish to emulate is to follow in their footsteps and mirror their behaviors. In following the example of Christ's suffering, we find ourselves on the best path to becoming more like Him in character as well. Paul briefly referenced this same idea at the end of our passage from the previous chapter: "I want to know Christ—yes, to know the power of his resurrection and participation in his sufferings, *becoming like him* in his death" (Philippians 3:10 NIV, emphasis added).

Paul communicates this even more clearly in a letter to the Corinthians, which we looked at back in chapter 3. In that chapter we examined how Paul views suffering as a key to gaining eternal perspective and to remembering our hope of eternal glory. It's within that very same letter we read these words:

> We are afflicted in every way, but not crushed; perplexed, but not driven to despair; persecuted, but not forsaken; struck down, but not destroyed; always carrying in the body the death of Jesus, so that the life of Jesus may also be manifested in our bodies (2 Corinthians 4:8-10).

I experience such an indescribable feeling when I see common threads woven and intertwined all throughout Scripture, pointing us to the same universal truths across multiple authors, locations, cultures, and experiences. In this chapter especially, I hope you are starting to see just how much these verses are crossing and connecting, as a tapestry of sorts takes shape before our eyes.

We began our study of biblical suffering with the difficult realization that there is no perfect way of living that can shield us from experiencing the pain inherent to the human experience. Now we see a deeper truth coming together as these same threads loop and intertwine: Attempting to avoid the suffering of this life isn't just impossible—it's actually detrimental to our faith. Just as we saw in the story of Jesus and the rich young ruler that a comfortable life is the largest barrier to gaining a kingdom perspective, we must now confront a similar theme among these teachings as well. If suffering holds the key to becoming more like Christ, isn't a life of comfort the greatest potential obstacle to our spiritual formation?

The irony here is all too glaring for me. I grew up in a church that sought to develop in me an indestructible faith that could survive any attack that might come my way, and yet I was also part of a congregation marked by incredible affluence and security. For all the ways the church warned me of the abstract trials of "persecution" I would face out in the secular world, there was no acknowledgment of the far more concrete barriers my faith could face from a life of prosperity and ease. Unfortunately, my experience in this church was far from unique; it is consistent with the practices of a majority of evangelical churches today. Systems of modern discipleship often follow the same misguided pattern: Create a space of safety, removed from the dangers of the world, where young believers have a chance to grow and nurture their faith, usually through Bible study, Scripture memorization, and a focus on righteous living.

Yet if we take these words of Peter, Paul, and James to heart, we are confronted with a difficult question: If suffering, pain, and persecution are the keys to developing our character and becoming more like Christ, how do we recognize and intentionally incorporate this into our practices of spiritual development? Obviously, we aren't going to start intentionally infecting students with Lyme disease at youth camp or advising our congregants to jump in front of a bus to better participate in the sufferings of Christ. Just as we saw Paul fight for the essential distinction between longing for heaven and being suicidal, we understand that there is equal danger in the extremes here as well. The question is how to seek out that holy place of tension in the middle, somewhere between the preservation of comfort and masochism.

I won't pretend to have a perfect answer to this question. Like most hard and holy pursuits, I don't believe there is a simple solution that somehow resolves the tension and files this issue away in a little box marked "solved." The first step here is simply to admit that this tension exists, and that we do in fact recognize how a life of comfort and privilege is ultimately detrimental to the formation of genuine faith. Standing squarely in the discomfort of the beliefs we struggle to comprehend always takes more wisdom than choosing to simply embrace the extreme that appeals more to us. Here is what I can say for certain: If we've already established that suffering is a universal human experience, that would suggest there won't be any need to seek out pain as an attempt to grow our faith. Pain is inevitable, and the trials will come; our task is discerning how to respond to them.

When we examined the account of Christ in the garden in the previous chapter, we also recognized that allowing suffering to develop our faith does not mean showing an attitude of cheerful indifference to our pain. I think this provides another essential clue as we seek out methods of effective discipleship. One of the more common practices used to try to inspire stronger faith is the sharing of testimonies. Modern testimonies tend to follow a similar pattern, where the speaker initially shares the details of some sort of trial they faced in the past. But—much like the classic sitcoms of our youth—the story always ends with the problem being solved, a lesson being learned, and every loose end tied neatly into a carefully crafted bow.

The goal of such testimonies is to give other believers a glimpse into God's power and faithfulness, convincing them to hang on and press forward until God shows up in power to give them their own testimonies of triumph. Yet when I look to Christ's example in the garden, I see something illuminating in the way He repeatedly tries to wake His disciples—not only so they could witness His suffering in its unpolished authenticity, before any happy ending or easy answers, but also so they could participate in His pain alongside him. Perhaps this example should inspire more present-tense testimonies, sharing our raw, unfinished stories of pain the same way we would share our past-tense triumphs. If the church developed a pattern of both inviting others into our pain and also willingly sharing in the pain of others, the opportunities for people to be shaped by suffering would only multiply.

Maybe this is the reason that, after we read about Paul declaring that "to live is Christ, and to die is gain" in Philippians 1:21, we find these words:

> Let each of you look not only to his own interests, but also to the interests of others. Have this mind among yourselves, which is yours in Christ Jesus, who, though he was in the form of God, did not count equality with God a thing to be grasped, but emptied himself, by taking the form of a servant, being born in the likeness of

men. And being found in human form, he humbled himself by becoming obedient to the point of death, even death on a cross (2:4-8).

If our own suffering is a powerful tool used to shape us into the image of Christ, how much more powerful could it be to follow His example here and run willingly into the suffering of others? In what greater way could we look to the interests of others, and what better opportunities could there be to empty ourselves and take on the form of servants, than in actively seeking to bear witness to the pain in our midst, faithfully holding space for those who mourn and lovingly choosing to share in the sufferings of others? I see ripples of this idea in Paul's letter to the Galatians: "Bear one another's burdens, and so fulfill the law of Christ" (6:2). I can't think of a stronger identifier of becoming Christlike than fulfilling His law.

Again, these threads weave and intersect and bring new dimension to our tapestry of suffering. Our pain becomes the link that carries us from mere Christian *orthodoxy*, having biblical beliefs, to true Christian *orthopraxy*, having Christlike practices and behaviors. Paul shows us in Romans that salvation by grace (orthodoxy) leads to hope, but that our suffering leads to the character (orthopraxy) that ultimately cements that hope. James shows us that participating in Christ's suffering doesn't only help us know Him more (orthodoxy), but actually transforms us to be more like Him, as evidenced by our behavior toward others (orthopraxy). In winding through these verses from Philippians and Galatians, we see Paul's reminders that Jesus not only willingly bore our burden on the cross to offer us salvation by grace (orthodoxy), but that we, too, are called to "bear one another's burdens, and so fulfill the law of Christ" (orthopraxy). If the question of modern discipleship is how to grow believers from a mere belief in Christ (orthodoxy) to a genuine faith that is both enduring and outwardly fruitful (orthopraxy), then suffering and learning to suffer well would appear to be the key.

If we return for a moment to Philippians 2, we see this illuminated in a whole new way: "Therefore, my beloved, as you have always obeyed, so now, not only as in my presence but much more in my absence, *work out your own salvation with fear and trembling*" (Philippians 2:12, emphasis added).

Now, Bible publishers usually separate chapters into smaller sections with titles labeling their different themes, and in my copy of the Bible, they separated out verses 1 through 11 as one segment and began a new segment with verse 12. It would have been easy to end my reading of our earlier passage at verse 11 and miss entirely what Paul says here. Likewise, I have seen verse 12 most commonly presented without any of the earlier context. It's helpful to remember that Philippians was originally a handwritten letter Paul sent to the church in Philippi, and these broken segments and subtitles didn't exist then.

Also, take special note of the word *therefore* at the beginning of this verse, which would suggest Paul is building directly on his previous thought. So, Paul directs us in earlier verses to consider the example of Christ humbly submitting Himself to bear our suffering, and he follows this thought with, "Therefore...work out your own salvation with fear and trembling" (2:12).

This has long been considered one of the most confusing, uncomfortable, and seemingly contradictory phrases in the New Testament. But, much like we saw with James 2:17 ("Faith by itself, if it does not have works, is dead"), a thread that seems brash and garish on its own takes on new beauty when it finds its perfect place in the greater tapestry. A proper theology of suffering reveals that this verse isn't a subversion of traditional orthodoxy, but rather a call to better orthopraxy. To put it another way, Paul doesn't tell them to work *for* their salvation, because he refers to it clearly as their "own," implying that it is something they already possess. Instead, he tells them to take the salvation they already possess and go work it out.

This is the very crux of discipleship: to work out our salvation the way we work out our biceps or quads. Paul offers a variation of the same truth he gave us in Romans 5:1-5, noting that just as our salvation by grace produces our glorious hope, the development of our endurance and character will strengthen and expand it.

Picture the example of biceps again. I *have* two biceps; they exist as part of my arms, and they really are mine. It would be a very different sentiment, however, to say, "Wow, she really *has some biceps!*" On the surface level, the sentence appears to say the same thing, but the meanings are entirely different. So, what is the key difference between these two kinds of "having"?

Working out helps us get the most from these muscles, rather than letting them simply take up space in our arms—and this eventually shows outwardly visible evidence of what was always inwardly true. Both concepts of "Work out your own salvation" (Philippians 2:12) and "Faith apart from works is dead" (James 2:26) get commonly misinterpreted as "Use it or lose it." But just as your biceps do not, in fact, disintegrate and cease to exist if you aren't regularly working out, neither Paul nor James claims your salvation is anything less than complete and secure in Christ. This was never meant to be about earning your salvation or working to keep it, but rather offering you a chance to take your inward beliefs and grow them into fruitful outward practices.

Woven throughout all these passages, written by different authors and to very different audiences, I see a singular, central theme. The experience of suffering, whether our own painful trials or the chance to follow in Christ's example to shoulder the suffering of others, is the best personal trainer for the muscle of our faith. As the church looks for successful models of discipleship and seeks to equip a new generation of believers with genuine and fruitful faith, a theology of suffering needs to play a vital role. It is only through suffering, and learning to suffer well, that we're able to work out our salvation successfully, shaping our spiritual body more into the form of Jesus, so that one day we "may be perfect and complete, lacking in nothing" (James 1:4).

....

As the church looks for successful models of discipleship and seeks to equip a new generation of believers with genuine and fruitful faith, a theology of suffering needs to play a vital role.

....

I ended the last chapter with a promise that, if you are willing to show up to your own bathroom floor or Gethsemane ground, Jesus will be faithful to meet you there inside your pain. I'm ending this chapter with an expansion of that same promise: Not only will He show up to meet you there, but He will grow your faith, stretch your endurance, produce new hope, and faithfully shape your character to become ever more like His. To borrow from Paul, "I am sure of this, that he who began a good work in you will bring it to completion at the day of Jesus Christ" (Philippians 1:6).

Chapter 6

Count It All Joy

The great theme of the Bible itself is how God brings
fullness of joy not just despite but through suffering...And
so there is a peculiar, rich, and poignant joy that seems
to come to us only through and in suffering.

TIMOTHY KELLER[1]

I recently listened to a recording of the first time I ever delivered a talk on suffering. I was hired to speak at a chapel service for Northwest Christian University, and I had actually prepared something really fun and upbeat on a different topic entirely. But two weeks before I was scheduled to speak, I had posted something to my blog that was uncharacteristically raw and revealing even for me. It was an unfiltered moment of sharing, posted on a whim before I gave it any second thought (or even any basic editing). The piece was simply titled "I've Been in Pain." Here's an excerpt of what I wrote:

> I've been neck deep in pain that was difficult to admit to myself, let alone to anyone else. It's a pain I've tried to rationalize myself out of, explain away, and stifle down in hopes it would disappear on its own. But as with most pain, it really doesn't work that way. It's continued on as this persistent ache, popping up at the most inopportune moments and gnawing away at my ability to ignore

it. It's not going anywhere, and the more I attempt to
ignore it the more aggravated it becomes.

I've been in pain.

At the beginning of 2015, in the midst of our multiple
months of unemployment, my husband and I discovered we were very unexpectedly pregnant. It was quite
the shock, and I would lying if I said it didn't take some
time to get used to the idea. It was literally the worst
possible timing, but it was far from unwelcome. We felt
blessed to be experiencing the possibility of another miracle baby, one we had been discussing for some time but
weren't quite ready to take the leap to try for yet. That
baby was a shining light in the middle of a dark season,
a much-needed anchor of hope to ballast us in the midst
of so much uncertainty.

And then, after a longer than usual ultrasound with the
nurse, the doctor said those horrible two words.

Not. Viable.

This marked the seventh child that we won't meet until
eternity. A seventh precious little one with no birthday
to celebrate, no future to plan.

I've been in pain.

Soon after the loss, my closest friend was blessed with
her own unexpected surprise: a fourth little one to join
her beautiful brood. It was a joy I admittedly have struggled to untangle from my own sorrow. The happiness I
feel for her is authentic, but it's difficult not to feel the
pain of the could have beens. Up until now all our boys
have been perfectly staggered in age. If I had carried my
most recent pregnancy to term, this trend would have

continued, but with the final pair being the closest in age of the bunch. We would have experienced our first pregnancy we'd actually get to do *together*. Watched the boys grow *together*. Done it all *together*.

I've been in pain.

Perhaps the hardest part of miscarriage is that the world around you goes on, and you carry no visible scar to help legitimize your pain. There isn't a label such as "widow." There is no grave marker to show. There are no words to properly explain the gaping hole you know you're walking around with but simply can't find a way to show. You're seemingly alone in it—and no one knows, or they've all but forgotten.

I've been in pain.

They say, "time heals all wounds." Has this ever really been true? If you leave a gaping hole in your leg untreated and wait for time to remedy it, does it really heal? Don't you usually end up with gangrene? Why have we been taught to believe any different with invisible wounds? Why do we beat ourselves up when our pain doesn't heal according to some fabricated timeline we've assigned ourselves? Why do we feel the need to limit the reaches of our grief? And how can we ever find healing for wounds we are so unwilling to admit, let alone treat.

I've been in pain.

My best friend welcomed her 4th little guy into the family a couple weeks ago. He's beautiful: perfect in every way. And with his birth, I was finally able to admit out loud to my husband for the first time what's really been paining me. Maybe it was the first time I was truly able

to admit it to myself. *I miss my baby.* I miss what might
have been. I ache to have a photo, or a birthday, or even
a name for this perfect little person I haven't been able
to meet.

I've been in pain.

Perhaps finally admitting it is the first step to *real* healing.
It stings like mad, but most wounds don't heal themselves. And I refuse to ignore this one any longer.[2]

It was less a blog post and more a journal entry, and by the next
morning I experienced what my friend Hannah brilliantly refers to
as a "vulnerability hangover." It's that moment when a writer realizes
that they have shared something profoundly personal and revealing, and that perhaps the world may see them very differently as
a result. I began to question whether it was wise to share so much,
and I seriously considered deleting the post to try and regain some
semblance of the brand I had worked to maintain on my blog. This
post came nestled between one about a sweet holiday tradition to try
to cultivate more contentment in my kids and an installment in an
empowering interview series, so it definitely lacked continuity with
the posts around it. Even the blog itself is called *The Joy Parade*, a
site branded with cheery hot-air balloons, bright pops of mint, and
whimsical Dalmatian prints, which all seem a stark contrast to the
pain I had shared.

The day after the piece went live, I received a call from Troy,
my contact at Northwest Christian. The call itself was expected,
since we were scheduled to finalize some details about my hotel stay
and what time we'd be meeting to set up. But Troy almost immediately mentioned the new blog post, which was entirely unexpected. I froze, my brain racing with concerns that the moment I
had pressed the button to share those words with the world, I may

have destroyed any semblance of professionalism or marketability as a speaker. No one would want to hear uplifting words of encouragement from the woman who was still neck-deep in grief over a loss that had taken place a year ago.

The voice on the other end of the phone was kind as Troy told me how sorry he felt for what I was going through, but then the conversation took its most surprising turn. He stumbled a bit at first—telling me he never really does this, and that ultimately the decision about what I would share in chapel would be mine alone—but he wondered if I might be willing to abandon the message I had already prepared and consider speaking specifically on the topic of pain and suffering instead.

However, the theme for their chapel services that year was the word *sacred*, and they were addressing questions of what is sacred and how we practice appropriate veneration and seek intentional space for holy things. I was worried about how I could manage to connect a message on suffering to that theme.

The theme was optional, Troy told me, and he went on to speak of how strongly he felt that I was uniquely equipped to bring something these students were desperately craving. "They get plenty of upbeat, inspirational messages," he said. "They don't often get someone willing to share from this sort of pain."

I spent the next two weeks taking some of the study I had been doing on the theology of suffering, everything God had shown me so far since that moment on the bathroom floor, and crammed it into a series of slides. And, because of what I'm convinced could only have been the Holy Spirit's leading, I decided to lean into the theme and title my message "Sacred Suffering."

Armed with only my slides of verses and a loose outline of what I was trying to say, I got up on that stage without my usual well-scripted plan. This talk would be in many ways as unfiltered as the blog post that led to it. I joked with my friend Edith that morning that I was just leaving a lot of extra room for the Holy Spirit, but it was much less a joke than a nervous realization. The Spirit could take this just about anywhere; I needed only to be faithful to show up and be willing.

What struck me most when I later listened to the audio recording of that chapel message wasn't how raw and vulnerable I was on stage, or how deeply apparent my pain was, but how much laughter took place throughout. Laughter! At a chapel service about the sacredness of our suffering, in the midst of a message laced with stories of crushing physical pain, trauma, loss, and grief, the audio is filled with so many periods of laughter.

The very idea of uproarious laughter during a message on sad and sacred topics probably sounds sacrilegious or offensive to most. When we think of venerating sacred things, we think of somber quiet. When we think of respecting grief and pain, we think of restrained tears and modest black attire. Yet here was a room full of students who connected deeply with what I was sharing, and as the space filled with tears, collective murmurs, and hums of knowing agreement, it also filled with equal parts giggles, guffaws, and outright laughter.

This was the most tangible time I have experienced the sacred existing in such an obvious tension of seeming contradictions. That experience was representative of a much larger quandary, though, a growing tension that existed not only in the confines of that one experience, but in my understanding of suffering on the whole. It is a tension you, too, may have noticed growing as you've read through these chapters so far, especially the previous one. The more we let ourselves go deeper in accepting and even embracing our pain, the more we see the word *joy* (or its verb form, *rejoice*) start to sneak its way into the biblical passages we study.

- "Rejoice insofar as you share Christ's sufferings, that you may also rejoice and be glad when his glory is revealed" (1 Peter 4:13).

- "Count it all joy, my brothers, when you meet trials of various kinds" (James 1:2).

- "We rejoice in our sufferings" (Romans 5:3).

In what is quite possibly the greatest of all the sacred contradictions we must wrestle with together, joy is inextricably tied to the theology of suffering. You might recall that the book of Philippians, a letter Paul wrote in chains, is a fairly short epistle compared to some of his others (only four chapters), and yet it contains more than ten separate uses of the noun *joy* (*chara* in Greek) or the verb *rejoice* (*chairō*). A letter from prison in which we read such difficult sentiments as "to live is Christ, and to die is gain" (1:21) is probably not the first place we would think to look while studying the idea of joy, and yet I firmly believe it's this very tension that makes it such an important place to start. Joy that comes easy, when life is good and blessings are in abundance, really isn't joy at all. That is happiness, an instinctual reaction to good circumstances. True joy, the kind we're speaking about here, is not dependent on circumstances—as apparent by its appearance in verses steeped in the themes of suffering and pain.

....

In what is quite possibly the greatest of all the sacred contradictions we must wrestle with together, joy is inextricably tied to the theology of suffering.

....

False Ideas

The question of how to find joy when you are suffering has been approached many times by many different writers, pastors, and teachers. One message I hear a lot is the idea that we are to endure a season of suffering to reach the reward of joy on the other side of our pain.

You've probably surmised that everything we've studied together so far poses a major challenge to this sort of teaching. We know that some pain is not temporary and will be with us until we reach eternity. We also know that even if we are relieved of our temporary pain here on earth, the season of pure joy these teachers promise is likely to be short lived, as new pains and griefs will come once more. This theology dooms some to a life without the possibility of joy because they will never reach the fabled "other side" of their pain. For others, it frames joy as a strange game of whack-a-mole: *Be sure to pounce quickly if you see joy pop up, because it will inevitably disappear again back down its hole, and you'll miss it if you don't move fast enough.*

Neither of these scenarios seems to embody the kind of joy Paul speaks of in Philippians though. Consider where he says, "Rejoice in the Lord always; again I will say, rejoice" (4:4). The word *always* is one of those words I would draw a small box around in my Bible for emphasis. I do this for words like *all, never,* or *everything* in order to draw my attention to words that are absolutes, words that communicate something all-inclusive and without exception. Paul tells us to rejoice in the Lord *always,* in all situations and without exceptions. But just to drive the point home, he then repeats himself again for emphasis. It's as if I were to say to you, "Whatever you do, never ever eat from this horrible food truck for the rest of your life. And don't eat there tomorrow either." Paul emphasizes the idea that *always* here is not some creative liberty, an exaggeration to make a

They say,
"Time heals all wounds."
Has this ever
really been true?
If you leave a gaping
hole in your leg
untreated and wait for
time to remedy it,
does it really heal?
Don't you usually end
up with gangrene?
Why have we been
taught to believe any
different with
invisible wounds?

point; this *always* quite literally means "always." So, if playing happiness "whack-a-mole" and waiting to pounce on fleeting moments of joy between our trials isn't what Paul teaches here, then what is he teaching?

The next most common answer I hear to the problem of finding joy in suffering is the mantra, "Choose joy." That mantra is rooted in a belief that affirms the existence of pain and suffering in this world, but stipulates that we always have a choice between letting suffering get to us or choosing a positive attitude instead. It's a theology that fits comfortably with other prosperity-gospel teachings, right between the "naming" and "claiming." The theme these responses all have in common? They put us, the believer, in the driver's seat. We can supposedly control the outcomes and our destiny because we can choose our way into the life that we're assured God will provide.

And yet, once again, we find another dead end. Not only can we identify the lies in this deeply transactional view of God, but we can also see how, through our study of Christ in the garden, the very notion that we could "just choose joy instead" ultimately falls short of His holy example of leaning into suffering. Moreover, the central idea here seems to be that our pain and joy are ends on a spectrum, and we must choose one or the other. But we have already seen so many examples of the most sacred things existing in holy tension between supposed contradictions.

The very reason so many lackluster teachings on joy fail in the end is because we can't experience or even understand true joy without laying the foundation of a healthy theology of suffering first. If I had begun this book with a chapter on joy, these false ideas of how to find joy when you're suffering might have seemed reasonable, and likely even appealing. Instead, I began this book on that bathroom floor, and we dove almost immediately into a spiritual "demolition day," tearing down everything we once held dear and replacing faulty beliefs with a new foundation. Everything we've built upon that foundation so far has given us the framework required to add a true and lasting joy into this new creation, and to easily identify the counterfeit pieces that simply could not fit with what's already here.

What is Paul's joy then? We know that he's not calling us to a joy that comes after, but a joy that comes *always*. We know he's not calling us to ignore our pain and "just choose joy," because he's so clearly shown us the power of embracing our suffering as the tool that not only draws us into deeper intimacy with Christ, but also makes us more like Him as it strengthens our faith and character. So how is it that Paul can call us to an ever-present joy while also teaching us to embrace our pain?

The kind of joy that Paul talks about, that true and lasting joy that transcends earthly circumstances, is the direct result of the very pain we've examined in previous chapters. Much like a newborn baby, this joy isn't birthed in spite of the painful labor; rather, the pain is an essential component of bringing forth that joy into the world.

In chapter 2 we learned that suffering is universal and unavoidable, a painful truth that may have felt much like a punch in the gut—as most early contractions do. Yet we finished that same chapter with a glimpse of the joy to come. We saw chains broken from the worry, guilt, and shame laid on us by a false belief that such suffering stems from a lack of faith or serves as a punishment for sin.

In chapter 3 we discovered that suffering is the key to an eternal view, allowing us to seek God's kingdom on earth while holding tightly to the promise of heaven. We saw a little more of the joy awaiting us, not only in the hope of the glory of heaven, but also in the recognition that our pain is never wasted, and God brings purpose to our most broken places.

In chapter 4 we found that our pain isn't a barrier between us and our relationship with Jesus, but rather a meeting place to connect with Him more intimately. We saw Christ's example in the garden and experienced the freedom of knowing that God never asks us to pretend everything is all right or to carry our suffering on our own in order to prove our worthiness for reward. Yet chapter 4 was heavy, and the pain seemed to intensify as we continued our study, much like it does in the difficult transition phase of labor as the baby is about to make its appearance at last.

Finally, in chapter 5 we learned that suffering doesn't only draw us into deeper intimacy with Christ, but it makes us more like Him, as well, while strengthening and developing us in ways nothing else can. This was the point in our time of labor that joy took its first breath with the words, "Count it all joy, my brothers, when you meet trials" (James 1:2).

The Secret to Enduring Joy

Everything we've studied together has been the labor that brought us here, as we've sought a true and abiding joy that exists not just *after* our suffering, but inside it, through it, and even because of it. It is at the very end of his letter to the Philippians that Paul leaves us his secret to experiencing this enduring joy. He begins by saying:

> Not that I am speaking of being in need, for I have learned in whatever situation I am to be content. I know how to be brought low, and I know how to abound. In any and every circumstance, I have learned the secret of facing plenty and hunger, abundance and need (Philippians 4:11-12).

Once again we see a picture of something much more radical than most modern notions of joy. Paul says he knows not only "how to abound," but "how to be brought low." He can rejoice not only in plenty, but in hunger—not only in abundance, but in need.

My focus in this passage went directly to the word *content*. Hungry to get a better understanding of what Paul means here, I went to the Greek for a look—and boy, was I met with a surprise. The specific Greek word that was translated here as *content* has only one appearance in all of the Bible, right here in this verse.

You may be thinking to yourself, *The Bible talks about contentment in other places, right?* Yes, it most certainly does, which is what immediately piqued my interest here. The Greek verb *arkeō* (ἀρκέω) is most commonly used to mean "to be content" or "to be sufficient."[3] (I realize this may be a bit confusing—since, in English, "content" is an adjective that we join with the verb "to be"—but Greek uses a single word to express person, number, tense, mood, voice, and action/state all in one self-contained verb.) This particular verb and its various conjugations appear eight times in the New Testament, including the following verses:

- "Keep your life free from love of money, and be content with what you have" (Hebrews 13:5).
- "If we have food and clothing, with these we will be content" (1 Timothy 6:8).
- "Be content with your wages" (Luke 3:14).

Without looking at the Greek, I would have assumed that Paul was speaking of this sort of contentment, a choice we make to accept that what we have is enough and to avoid the greed of asking for more. And yet the unique word he chose points to something deeper.

The word Paul actually uses here is *autarkēs*, and it's an adjectival combination of the word *arkeō* (that we looked at above) and the word *autos*, meaning "self." One definition for *autarkēs* is "sufficient for one's self, strong enough or possessing enough to need no aid or support."[4] I found that odd and tried reading back through the passage with the translation "self-sufficient" in place of "content," but I could not make sense of it.

Then I peeked ahead to the next verse and saw one of the most famous lines in Scripture: "I can do all things through him who strengthens me" (Philippians 4:13). It's a verse you might be surprised to encounter on a study focused on suffering, because it's been so commonly used in prosperity-gospel teachings. Worried about passing that English exam you didn't really study enough for? "Just pray on it; you can do *all* things in Christ." Your spouse is concerned that a certain career move would be risky and unwise? "They just need more faith, because we can do *all* things in Christ." Philippians 4:13 has become the theme for Christian sports camps, been emblazoned across posters of climbing Mount Everest, and even found its way into my inbox as part of a campaign to encourage women to sign up for a multilevel marketing company. It has been used less as a verse of Scripture and more as a cheesy inspirational mantra.

Take a small detour with me for a minute to another letter of Paul's that we have looked at before, 2 Corinthians. Here we find Paul talking about contentment and making reference to his strength in Christ. This passage reveals Paul's secret to abiding joy.

> He said to me, "My grace *is sufficient* for you, for my power is made perfect in weakness." Therefore I will boast all the more gladly of my weaknesses, so that the power of Christ may rest upon me. For the sake of Christ, then, I am *content* with weaknesses, insults, hardships, persecutions, and calamities. For when I am weak, then I am strong (2 Corinthians 12:9-10, emphasis added).

I emphasized the phrase "is sufficient" at the beginning of the passage, because the word used there is *arkeō* (ἀρκέω), which we looked at earlier. I also emphasized the word *content*, but the word used here isn't actually connected to any of the other Greek words we have looked at so far. This term is something new entirely.

The word used here is *eudokeō* (εὐδοκέω). This word is a combination of *eu* (εὖ), meaning "to be well off, fare well, prosper"[5] and *dokeō* (δοκέω), meaning "to be of opinion, think, suppose."[6] Thus, *eudokeō* means to "think it good" or "to be well pleased with."[7] In fact, when God famously announces from heaven, "This is my beloved Son, with whom *I am well pleased*" (Matthew 3:17, emphasis added), it's this word that is used.

With this brief detour into the Greek in mind, I want to return to the Corinthians passage once more with fresh eyes. In the preceding verses, Paul pleads with God to remove a "thorn in the flesh," a source of suffering in his life of which we don't know the specifics. Verse 9 is God's response: "My grace is sufficient for you, for my power is made perfect in weakness." We might paraphrase the first part as saying, "You can be content in My grace as being enough for you."

Paul takes these words from the Lord to heart, embracing his weakness and the suffering of this persistent thorn, and says something profound in verse 10: "For the sake of Christ, then, I am content with weaknesses, insults, hardships, persecutions, and calamities. For when I am weak, then I am strong." With our look at the Greek in mind, we could read this as saying, "For the sake of Christ, then, I am [*well pleased*] with weaknesses, insults, hardships, persecutions, and calamities."

All throughout this passage we see two threads being woven together: contentedness and weakness. Paul finds the key to a content spirit not in keeping a gratitude journal or in seeking out the simple life and its quiet pleasures, but in recognizing and accepting his own weakness. That weakness, one he ties directly to experiencing "insults, hardships, persecutions, and calamities," in turn becomes the key to strength, as God's power is made perfect in our weakness. This is a radical picture of Paul finding contentment not in spite of his lack, but because of it. The more he willingly allows himself to be emptied, the more God imbues that empty vessel with His perfect strength. It's with this in mind that we can read those closing thoughts to the Philippians with new insight on that previously puzzling "self-sufficient" word.

> Not that I am speaking of being in need, for I have learned in whatever situation I am *to be content* [or "self-sufficient"]. I know how to be brought low, and I know how to abound. In any and every circumstance, I have learned the secret of facing plenty and hunger, abundance and need. I can do all things through him who strengthens me (Philippians 4:11-13, emphasis added).

Why would Paul use a word for being self-sufficient when he points to this contentment as the secret to having abiding joy in the face of his trials? The answer lies in verse 13, because he "can do all things through [God] who strengthens [him]." When I read these words in a Greek parallel Bible, I saw *panta ischyō en toi endynamounti me* next to their most literal translation in English, "All things I am strong for in the One strengthening me."[8] Seeing this version helps make it clear just how much the emphasis was never supposed to be on the "I can do" part of this verse. The more literal translation makes our part so much more passive than in the familiar memory-verse mantra. In this version, God gets the only real action verb, *strengthening*, and the only verb pertaining to Paul (and us) is the word *am,* which grammar poignantly classifies as a "state of being" verb.

Philippians 4:13 is less a verse about *doing* all the things, and more about *enduring* them. When Paul speaks of self-sufficiency, he does so with the understanding that what is inside him is ultimately Christ. The empty vessel he became for the sake of Christ is now filled to sufficiency with the power of His strength.

Paul's secret to finding joy in suffering isn't a method to better overcome our pain or even a way to strengthen us against its effects. No, Paul's secret is acceptance and surrender. Paul isn't offering a binary choice between feeling the pain or choosing joy; he's calling us to run headfirst into our pain with the radical belief that it's the very wellspring from which our greatest joy abounds.

Of all the contradictions we've had to grapple with in this book, this is by far the most difficult. Paul tells us that the way to experience true and abiding joy that isn't dependent on our circumstances is to embrace our insufficiency, let go of striving, and give ourselves over to the One whose strength is made perfect in our weakness.

Filled with Joy

Imagine that you have an exceptionally tight monthly budget, and every week you sit with your bills and your bank ledger, frantically trying to keep your head above water. It seems like every week there is a new surprise expense, and it feels like this whole precariously balanced house of cards will come down at any moment, and you'll lose everything.

Your friends see you consumed by stress, and they encourage you to seek out ways to find more joy. One suggests you should get yourself a massage. "Practice a little self-care," she says. You consider it, but all you can think about is how the cost of that luxury will likely result in an overdrawn bank account when the next bills hit. Another friend suggests you start a gratitude journal, advising you to write down only the things you are grateful for and let go of obsessing over the spreadsheets for a while. She's well-meaning enough, but you wonder if she knows how much she's invalidating your very real concerns. You cannot simply ignore your budget, because if you do, it is very likely that you will miss something important and cause even bigger problems in the long run. Plus, no matter how much you try to think about what you are grateful for, it doesn't ultimately change your financial circumstances in the end.

Then one day you drive to work, and your car breaks down. You call the mechanic only to discover that you need a serious repair equal in cost to your entire monthly income. You collapse on the curb in defeat and, with tears in your eyes, call your bank to tell them you just can't manage anymore. You ask them to advise you on how to file for bankruptcy. You're done fighting, you're done scraping, you just can't deal with it anymore.

Now, picture what would happen if the voice on the other end of the line were to say, "This is wonderful. Now that you've let go and accepted your inability to handle this on your own, the bank would be happy to step in to get you caught up. Not only that, but we'd like to start covering all your expenses from this point forward, indefinitely. We'll put through all the necessary paperwork on our end right now. Have a great day!" Can you even imagine? How would you react? What would it feel like having that burden lifted, experiencing that moment of total freedom? I, for one, am pretty sure I would be singing and dancing right there on the sidewalk from pure elation.

This is the very freedom Paul calls us into, his secret to an abiding joy that transcends all circumstances. Our greatest suffering brings us to our moments of greatest weakness, and it's in that same weakness that the power of Christ is made perfect in us. The more we feel empty, the more we can be filled to the brink with the sufficiency of Christ. Recognizing that truth and embracing that sufficiency bring a freedom that releases us from every burden, causing the most immeasurable joy. It's not a joy we chase or attempt to somehow fabricate; it's a joy we simply open our empty hands to receive.

Think again about the bank story: If you were to have another large, unexpected expense hit the following month, could it in any way steal from your newfound joy? No, because the bank said they would cover your expenses, so nothing you could face would add to or subtract from the total you owed. It would always be zero! Such is our sufficiency in Christ. Our joy cannot be taken from us by our circumstances, because His grace is sufficient for us, His power made perfect in our weakness.

When I gave that message on suffering at Northwest Christian University, I was only able to inspire such genuine laughter because I had already experienced my bathroom floor moment and met Christ with my white flag of defeat. In turn, He had filled me so sufficiently that my joy spilled out all over the place. I had to perch on a stool that day because my chronic fatigue was so debilitating, and my nerve pain was so intense that I wasn't sure I could make it through the entire talk without falling over. *But my joy was full.* My Lyme was still undiagnosed at that point, so I was living under a cloud of confusion and frustration because we had no explanation for why my body was seemingly shutting down. *But my joy was full.* My family was absolutely drowning financially, in large part because of the costs of my medical care, and we were facing the very real possibility of losing our home. *But my joy was full.* My grief was still so tangible, and when I shared about the seven children I was mourning, the room was filled with faces streaked with tears. *But my joy was still full.*

That's the thing about true joy: It doesn't exist on a spectrum, opposite our pain. Joy doesn't replace our pain; joy simply *redeems* it. Too often we see our grief or sorrow as evidence that joy hasn't reached us. We read that there is "a time to weep, and a time to laugh; a time to mourn, and a time to dance" (Ecclesiastes 3:4), and we assume that these seasons are separate and self-contained. I've found, however, that these seasons usually overlap and intertwine, the bitter and the sweet poured together in the same cup. That's part of the mystery: that grief and joy, faith and fear, weakness and power all exist in an intimate dance until you can hardly tell where one begins and one ends. It's friends laughing over old memories while gathered for a funeral. It's a couple sharing a night of intimacy after recently losing a loved one. It's a family having sweet experiences at Disneyland while facing a cancer diagnosis. It's celebrating your best friend's wedding while you are getting a divorce.

....

True joy doesn't exist on a spectrum, opposite our pain. Joy doesn't replace our pain; joy simply *redeems* it.

....

Nowhere in Scripture do I see this more clearly than in the book of Psalms. Remember David's great lament, "My God, my God, why have you forsaken me?" That's found in Psalm 22 (verse 1), right before the famous Psalm 23, which begins, "The LORD is my shepherd; *I shall not want*" (verse 1, emphasis added). For every line in which we see David celebrating God's beauty and His abundant blessings, there is another dripping with pain and raw grief—and yet David served the same faithful and present God throughout. Therein lies the beauty of Psalms: joy and pain, gratitude and lament, all finding their place together as David chased faithfully after God's heart. And in seeking to know God as intimately as possible, David found the same enduring joy that Paul would find so many years later:

> Preserve me, O God, *for in you I take refuge.* I say to the Lord, "You are my Lord; *I have no good apart from you*"…Therefore my heart is glad, and my whole being rejoices; my flesh also dwells secure…You make known to me the path of life; *in your presence there is fullness of joy*; at your right hand are pleasures forevermore (Psalm 16:1-2,9,11, emphasis added).

The very same fullness of joy that both David and Paul experienced is available to each and every one of us. As you read the following words of Jesus, my prayer is that you would embrace your weakness and fall freely into the ever-present arms of Christ.

> Abide in me, and I in you. As the branch cannot bear fruit by itself, unless it abides in the vine, neither can you, unless you abide in me. I am the vine; you are the branches. Whoever abides in me and I in him, he it is that bears much fruit, for apart from me you can do nothing…*These things I have spoken to you, that my joy may be in you, and that your joy may be full* (John 15:4-5,11, emphasis added).

It is only when we submit ourselves wholly as empty vessels that we can be filled by Christ and find abiding joy.

Chapter 7

Cover Your Mirrors

He's inviting me to heal, but also to see my most meaningful calling: to be His healing to the hurting. My own brokenness, driving me into Christ's, is exactly where I can touch the brokenhearted.

Ann Voskamp[1]

In the week after the horrific tragedy at Charlottesville in 2017, I made an extraordinary discovery about who I am. It was the worst kind of irony, because as my social media feed filled with the terrifying images of men with torches chanting, "Jews will not replace us," I learned for the first time that I am a Jewish woman myself.

I was adopted at age three, and to complicate matters even further, my birth mother was actually adopted herself. My genealogy was a complete mystery my whole life, and as a little girl I had so desperately craved an identity of my own that I had somehow decided I was half-French and half-Italian—something I had repeated to myself so many times I had almost forgotten it was pure imagination. But in the week after Charlottesville my birth mother told me an incredible story, one she had only recently learned herself.

Years ago, there had been two families: one of proud Irish Catholics, and the other a devout Jewish family with strong Orthodox roots. In a story that sounds exactly like a made-for-TV modern adaptation of *Romeo and Juliet*, the young Jewish girl fell into a forbidden love with the dashing Irish Catholic boy, and they eloped, as their families would certainly never allow their union. Only, this story had a twist: my birth mother, their child.

Once the pregnancy was discovered, the families were in total upheaval. The couple was separated, and the families instructed an adoption agency that, once the child was born, he or she was only to be placed with a Protestant Christian couple—the closest thing to a compromise they could come up with. As was common with adoptions in her day, my birth mother grew up without any information about her parents or her history, and so it was a total surprise for both of us to finally learn the details of our shared past. In the Jewish tradition, Jewish heritage is actually passed on not from the fathers, but via the matrilineal line. Under Jewish law, my grandmother passed her Jewish identity to my birth mother, who in turn passed it to me, and I in turn have passed it to my sons. In fact, there are numerous charities and organizations that help fund trips for people like myself to return to Israel and learn more about their culture and heritage.

As much as this discovery was a complete surprise, it felt less like a disruption and more like a homecoming. For years I had felt unusually drawn to aspects of Jewish faith and history and had somehow felt strangely connected to stories of the Jewish people, but I had usually written this off as some kind of misled evangelical notion of seeing ourselves as "God's new chosen people" today. Perhaps my heart somehow always understood what my brain could not possibly have known. This was always a part of who I am, a sacred history imprinted in my very DNA and a thread connecting me through time to the people of Israel.

Since learning about my heritage, I've spent a lot of time studying Jewish culture and tradition, especially in regard to the Jewish faith. One of the areas I've been most drawn to is the traditional practices of Jewish mourning. The Jewish people have endured a long history of suffering, and this has produced a rich and deep theology around themes like pain, grief, and lament. One of the things most evident in this tradition is that the Jewish people view suffering communally. In white, westernized cultures, we tend to see suffering in deeply individualized ways, regarding pain as uniquely personal and even private in many cases. However, Jewish culture treats grief as a communal practice, and many of the traditional observances of mourning reflect this idea.

When a Jewish person is buried, the family of the deceased will begin an initial seven-day process of mourning known as "sitting shiva."[2] In fact, *shiva* literally means "seven." There are a number of rules about how a mourner is to approach grooming and appearance during a period of shiva, all of them designed to make a mourner easy for the community to identify by bringing their outward appearance into alignment with their inward dishevelment. The mourners also sit on small stools or boxes, positioned very low to the ground, symbolizing that they have been "brought low" emotionally by their grief. Sitting in these seats is visibly uncomfortable, which again serves to demonstrate outwardly the pain of their inward state.

During shiva the mourning family will leave their front door unlocked, and visitors from the community are encouraged to visit them without any invitation. In fact, the mourners do not traditionally invite anyone over into their home, prepare refreshments, or otherwise host their guests in the way we typically see in Western culture. The only job of the mourners during shiva is to grieve, and the community is expected to hold space faithfully with them in this time. This idea is so important that visitors actually are expected not to initiate conversations with the mourners, but simply to converse among themselves and wait, patiently available, unless and until the mourners themselves desire to speak.

When this seven-day period ends, the community brings the mourners into their next phase of grief (known as *sheloshim*) by helping them literally rise from their low-seated positions and escorting them on a symbolic walk around the block to announce their reentry into the daily routines of the community. It is impossible for mourners to be invisible in these traditions, and the community is consistently pressed, not only to recognize the grieving in their midst, but to minister to their unique needs as they mourn.

Yet, for all the ways the community is expected to focus on the mourners, the mourners are surprisingly directed to focus outside themselves as well. The most common words of condolence offered to a mourner sitting shiva are, "May God comfort you among all the mourners of Zion and Jerusalem." It's a concept that seems contrary to our Western ideas of grief, and my guess is that this may even seem a bit offensive to you. We love the "may God comfort you" piece, but bristle at the "among all the mourners" part of the blessing. Isn't it invalidating to offer supposed comfort by taking someone's unique pain and dropping it into this larger bucket of common experience? More importantly, how can we ask someone in a period of such deep sorrow to consider the pain of anyone else but themselves?

But that's not all. In probably the most famously known observance of sitting shiva, every mirror in the home of the mourner is often covered, and they are expected to refrain from tending to their personal appearance with habits like shaving or applying makeup. This, too, seems to oppose our Western ideas of mourning. We commonly tell those experiencing this kind of loss to focus on themselves and give themselves extra self-care in this difficult time. Yet Jewish tradition dictates quite the opposite, with various observances that specifically ask mourners to deny themselves, while also pointing them outward to the grief of so many others both in their community and in the larger history of the Jewish people.

The beauty of Jewish mourning is this: In first making the community responsible for the mourners, they not only make it possible for the mourners to focus entirely outside themselves, but also to seek healing and purpose there as well. When we are wholly responsible for one another, there is no longer a need for self-care, because our needs are fully met by our community. Grief in the Western world can be incredibly isolating, whereas grief in the Jewish tradition is a constant reminder that we all belong to one another. As the community holds space for the mourners, the mourners in turn are able to resist the temptation to be inwardly consumed by their own pain. And in sharing in the comfort of their community, they are reminded of the way their pain also ties them back to that same community as well.

Find Deep Belonging

Consider these words from the apostle Paul:

> Blessed be the God and Father of our Lord Jesus Christ, the Father of mercies and God of all comfort, who comforts us in all our affliction, so that we may be able to comfort those who are in any affliction, with the comfort with which we ourselves are comforted by God. For as we share abundantly in Christ's sufferings, so through Christ we share abundantly in comfort too. If we are afflicted, it is for your comfort and salvation; and if we are comforted, it is for your comfort, which you experience when you patiently endure the same sufferings that we suffer. Our hope for you is unshaken, for we know that as you share in our sufferings, you will also share in our comfort (2 Corinthians 1:3-7).

We saw in chapter 4 how, in suffering, Christ offers not only the possibility of a deeper connection with us, but also a more perfect comfort for us as well. Paul takes this same truth a step further, connecting us not only back to Christ, but outward to our community as well. He beautifully illuminates these themes of suffering and comfort as if they are partners in an intimate dance, spinning together in a way that cannot possibly be untangled, while also blurring the lines between ourselves and the other members in our community. He says in verse 6, "If we are afflicted, it is for your comfort...and if we are comforted, it is for your comfort." Just like the shiva traditions, Paul gives us a picture of a community that belongs wholly to one another and reminds us that inside our pain is where we experience this most clearly.

· ·

> When we are wholly responsible
> for one another, there is no longer a
> need for self-care, because our needs
> are fully met by our community.

· ·

But, much like the traditions of shiva, Paul also calls us to turn our focus away from ourselves as individuals and outward to that shared community. Remember in chapter 5 when we read in Paul's letter to the Philippians, "Let each of you look not only to his own interests, but also to the interests of others" (2:4)? Think back further now to chapter 3, when we saw him wrestling with even heavier ideas like "to live is Christ, and to die is gain" (1:21). Do you find it hard to believe that these two radically different verses appear fairly close together in that same letter? Let's take a look at what comes between them, as Paul walks us through his own process of turning his focus outward.

To me to live is Christ, and to die is gain. If I am to live
in the flesh, that means fruitful labor for me. Yet which I
shall choose I cannot tell. I am hard pressed between the
two. My desire is to depart and be with Christ, for that
is far better. *But to remain in the flesh is more necessary on
your account. Convinced of this, I know that I will remain
and continue with you all, for your progress and joy in the
faith, so that in me you may have ample cause to glory in
Christ Jesus,* because of my coming to you again (1:21-26,
emphasis added).

We begin with Paul vulnerably disclosing his own longing for
heaven, a desire to be free of his earthly pain and in the presence of
Christ. It's easy to see how an inward focus could cause Paul to be
consumed by the weight of his own suffering, and how fixating too
fully on that longing for heaven could cause him to lose grip on any
meaning for life here on earth.

However, Paul has a community of believers in Philippi who are
devotedly holding space for him, and in caring for him faithfully in
this time of suffering (see 4:14-18), they have created the very tether
that pulls him out of himself and into a spirit of purpose. He says in
no uncertain terms that he belongs to them, choosing to focus on
the calling of someday ministering again to those who are currently
ministering to him, "so that in [him they] may have ample cause to
glory in Christ Jesus" (verse 26).

Continuing further into the passage, we read:

Only let your manner of life be worthy of the gospel of
Christ, so that whether I come and see you or am absent,
I may hear of you that you are standing firm in one
spirit, with one mind striving side by side for the faith
of the gospel, and not frightened in anything by your

opponents. This is a clear sign to them of their destruction, but of your salvation, and that from God. For it has been granted to you that for the sake of Christ you should not only believe in him but also suffer for his sake, engaged in the same conflict that you saw I had and now hear that I still have (1:27-30).

The next couple verses after verse 26 seem to take a detour as Paul talks briefly about seeking unity in the body, but then the passage returns to Paul's familiar theme of suffering together for the sake of Christ. In reading on, we discover those seemingly out of place urgings toward unity are not a detour at all.

> So if there is any encouragement in Christ, any comfort from love, any participation in the Spirit, any affection and sympathy, complete my joy by being of the same mind, having the same love, being in full accord and of one mind. Do nothing from selfish ambition or conceit, but in humility count others more significant than yourselves. Let each of you look not only to his own interests, but also to the interests of others (2:1-4, emphasis added).

Here Paul clearly ties experiencing comfort and encouragement right back to this theme of belonging to one another in community, by "having the same love, being in full accord and of one mind" (verse 2). He doesn't stop there though. He continues on to urge us back outside ourselves even more explicitly, with the call to give up all selfishness or self-focus and to consider the interests of others.

Paul has, in essence, laid out a road map, a path from a grief so heavy that we can't help but long for heaven, to a place where we experience encouragement, comfort, love, and joy—all wrapped up in a community of deep belonging. He does this first by demonstrating his own outward shift of focus, and then by calling us to that same shift as well.

Put more simply, Paul calls us to *cover our mirrors*. Yet, just as the traditions of shiva do not hide or minimize the very real grief of the mourner, Paul is in no way suggesting that we should simply hide away our pain and put on a brave face for those around us. He points instead to a far more radical idea: that when we acknowledge and even embrace our deepest pain, we find a springboard to our greatest calling, if only we can turn our focus outward.

Practice Love

For most of my life I struggled greatly with low self-esteem—so much so that it would be far more accurate to say I struggled with a deep sense of hatred for myself. This was compounded by horrible social anxiety, despite being incredibly extroverted and seemingly outgoing. No matter how social I may have appeared, though, I was running through a never-ending internal dialogue of suspicions and fears. *Oh God, I'm always talking too much. Everyone is wishing I would just shut up already...Come on, Stephanie, you know they don't actually like you; they only tolerate you to be polite...I wonder what they all say about me when I'm not around. Do they laugh at how oblivious I am to being so unwanted? Am I just a running joke to everyone?* Outwardly I would laugh and joke, endlessly talking about one thing or another, but once I would reach the silence of my car or the privacy of a restroom stall, I would berate myself through hot tears for being too much.

I spent so many years trying to work on these issues in therapy: reading books on self-esteem, doing topical Bible studies, and attempting anything I could to correct this problem. I tried physically surrounding myself with positive affirmations, sticking them on note cards and brightly colored Post-it notes all around my room and car. I would try to meditate on themes like "I am fearfully and wonderfully made" or "I am worthy of love." But no matter how much I tried to build up my self-esteem, nothing seemed to make any kind of significant impact.

One night at a Christian women's retreat I recounted the saga of this lifelong struggle to a good friend and tearfully exhaled the words, "I just don't want to hate myself anymore." As the words left my mouth I expected to be drawn into a familiar hug of encouragement, where I could be baptized anew with a stream of loving affirmations. Instead, my dear friend looked me straight in the eyes and, with equal parts tenderness and authority, said, "Stephanie, I love you enough to tell you the truth. If you really want to stop being so all-consumed by this self-hatred and anxiety, I don't think you need to learn how to think of yourself more highly; I think you need to learn how to think of yourself *less*."

The words stung so fiercely that they felt like a physical slap to the face. My cheeks burned red with anger and embarrassment, and the competing urges of fight and flight were so deadlocked that I sat unable to formulate any response at all. She slid in closer to me on the small couch, pulled out a copy of *The Message* from her bag, and asked if she could read me something from her quiet time that morning.

> My dear children, let's not just talk about love; let's practice real love. This is the only way we'll know we're living truly, living in God's reality. It's also the way to shut down debilitating self-criticism, even when there is something to it. For God is greater than our worried hearts and knows more about us than we do ourselves. And friends, once that's taken care of and we're no longer

accusing or condemning ourselves, we're bold and free
before God! (1 John 3:18-21 MSG).

There it was, right there in black and white, "the way to shut
down debilitating self-criticism, even when there is something to
it." What was that seemingly elusive secret? To not just talk about
love, but to practice real love so fiercely, and in a way that's so all-
consuming, that we are too busy being the hands and feet of Jesus to
hate ourselves anymore. It is when we turn our focus outward, fully
committing our time and attention to how best to love the people
around us, that we are finally able to stop accusing or condemning
ourselves, and instead live "bold and free before God."

What felt like an insult had been the words of a true friend, one
who loved me fiercely enough to try to guide me out of my struggle
once and for all. She knew that if she continued to feed me positive
affirmations, I would still be focusing on myself, a focus that would
inevitably lead me to notice my own flaws and failures once again—
which was exactly why all my previous attempts to end this cycle
had failed. The answer I so desperately sought, the way to point me
toward a lasting healing and a life of true freedom, was to look outside myself entirely.

Whether the suffering we're dealing with is our own debilitating self-hatred, a grief so deep that our longing for heaven feels it
could untether us from earth, or a different sort of pain entirely, the
path to healing is ultimately the same. When we turn the focus of
our pain off ourselves and out to our community, we take the very
experiences meant for our harm and turn them into tools for growing the kingdom. The prophet Isaiah spoke of turning "swords into
plowshares" (2:4) as a sign of God's kingdom yet to come, and I can't
help but see a parallel in turning the weapons of pain and suffering
into tools to build up His kingdom here on earth.

When we turn
the focus of our
pain off ourselves
and out to our
community, we
take the very
experiences meant
for our harm and
turn them into
tools for growing
the kingdom.

Consider the Jewish traditions of mourning again. Here we can see a community walking this out so well that they have managed to take one of the greatest curses of death, the severing of that sacred bond of human connection, and somehow turn that pain into a powerful tool to deepen and strengthen their connections to one another. Despite each individual being asked to forgo a focus on their own needs, no one is left with their needs unmet, because each is being pointed to care faithfully for the other, and the whole community is strengthened as these acts of love bind them together.

Refocus the Pain

It's vital to understand that we aren't talking about simply ignoring our pain by trying to distract ourselves with volunteerism. There is an old joke where a man calls his doctor and says, "I'm looking in my bathroom mirror right now, and there is some kind of horrible sore right in the middle of my forehead! It doesn't hurt, but it looks terrible, and I can see it oozing. What should I do?" To which the doctor replies, "Have you tried turning off the bathroom light?"

It is a ridiculous joke, but it would be equally ridiculous to think that simply ignoring our own hurts could bring any kind of meaningful healing either. Ignoring a wound does not lead to healing; it leads to gangrene—and our emotional wounds are no exception. Think again of the shiva traditions. Imagine how different the outcome would be if mourners were told to pull themselves together after the burial, immediately head back to work, and just focus on being so busy they can hardly remember their loved one has died. Would this bring any kind of meaningful healing? In the same way, if we try to seek this outward focus on its own, divorced from a rich and meaningful theology of suffering, we won't invite healing— only neglected wounds ripe for festering infections.

The key difference here is that it's not enough to simply focus our attentions elsewhere; true healing comes when we refocus our pain itself. This healing isn't someone spending weekends volunteering at soup kitchens to avoid the pain of an empty house after losing a spouse; it is a man I watched experience the fullness of that heartbreak and then channel his pain outward to create Saturday meetups for other men who are widowed or divorced. It is not a woman putting on a cheerful facade each Mother's Day service as she walks through infertility; it is the woman I know who used her experiences to reach out to churches and offered resources she created to show others how they can faithfully hold space for those experiencing similar pain. It is not someone trying to overcome depression by visiting terminal patients in order to guilt herself into more gratefulness; it is my friend who vulnerably published a memoir about her own mental health struggles in an effort to erase the stigmas and bring hope to others waging a similar war. It is not the deeply toxic suggestion that victims should "forgive and forget" horrific acts of abuse; it is my friend who bravely went public with her story of sexual abuse by a former pastor and began passionately advocating for necessary change in churches all around the country.

Healing is not about distracting ourselves from our pain, because it is only when we accept our pain that we can repurpose it as a meaningful tool for ministry—turning those swords into plowshares.

This book is my plowshare, each word an attempt to turn my personal pain into a valuable tool of purpose. I think of the words of Paul, who, after enduring horrible treatment (see Acts 16:11-40; 17:1-15), writes a letter to the church in Thessalonica, to believers who are enduring the same sorts of persecution he has experienced. He says to them, "Being affectionately desirous of you, *we were ready to share with you not only the gospel of God but also our own selves*, because you had become very dear to us" (1 Thessalonians 2:8, emphasis added). That is my goal for this book, to share not only the gospel of God, but also my own self, which requires a willingness not only to reopen old wounds, but also to allow myself to experience new ones more fully.

The very week I sat down to write this chapter, my family suffered the devastating loss of my dear cousin Brent to an unusually aggressive form of leukemia. He was only 25, an exceptionally vibrant young man brimming with potential and an unparalleled zest for life. Brent shared a special bond with my son Aidan, something that transcended the usual challenges of Aidan's autism and brought him so much growth and emotional development. He idolized Uncle Brent, and we could not have dreamed of a better role model for our boys. His death has left us all feeling bewildered and overwhelmed in its wake, and grief has been like a thick fog hanging heavy over our home.

The process of forcing myself to show up to these pages has provided an invaluable chance to walk out what I'm writing about in a whole new way, allowing me to apply these truths in the very present tense. I understand so much more clearly why Paul pointed to that connection with others as the tether that anchored him, how it grounded him to earth when the pull of heaven grew so strong. This chapter essentially became my own version of that shiva blessing, "May God comfort you among all the mourners of Zion and Jerusalem." In writing these pages I am reminded that, like the shiva mourners, the grief I am experiencing is not unique or isolating; rather, these sacred ties of suffering connect me all the more deeply to so many others.

I don't know the details of your own pain, but I can promise you that there is no suffering powerful enough to stand outside the reach of God's redemption. Paul writes, "We know that for those who love God all things work together for good, for those who are called according to his purpose" (Romans 8:28). I think it's vital to address that far too often this verse is used to suggest that God orchestrates our suffering because it's somehow for our betterment. This theology is often accompanied with inaccurate platitudes like "Everything happens for a reason" and encouragement to try to find the "lesson" in every tragedy or injustice. It's important to understand that finding healing, redemption, and even purpose inside our suffering is not synonymous with finding a *reason* or an *explanation* for our pain. Those answers are something we were never guaranteed to find on this side of eternity, and this verse shouldn't be misconstrued as a promise that we as Christians will always be able to make sense of our afflictions.

When connected to a healthy theology of suffering, though, Romans 8:28 offers a much fuller promise. It's a powerful declaration that there is nothing in this world that can derail the final will of God, and that no pain you experience, no loss you endure, no mistakes you make, and no evil that is ever done to you could ever rob you of His promises or His presence.

Paul goes on to further clarify that very truth just a few verses later:

> Who shall separate us from the love of Christ? Shall tribulation, or distress, or persecution, or famine, or nakedness, or danger, or sword?...No, in all these things we are more than conquerors through him who loved us. For I am sure that neither death nor life, nor angels nor rulers, nor things present nor things to come, nor powers, nor height nor depth, nor anything else in all creation, will be able to separate us from the love of God in Christ Jesus our Lord (Romans 8:35,37-39).

Friend, there is no suffering great enough to remove you from

God's hand. There is no pain deep enough to rob you of the hope of heaven. There is no evil powerful enough to destroy the promise that one day God will finally restore every broken thing to triumphant perfection. So when we pray, "Your kingdom *come*, your will be done, *on earth as it is in heaven*" (Matthew 6:10, emphasis added), we are boldly asking to see pieces of that glorious someday redemption arrive in the here and now. It's a prayer I've seen faithfully answered time and time again, and yet I admit that it still confounds me. God does not orchestrate this suffering or deliberately bring us pain, and yet somehow He still redeems it for good. He absolutely did not "will" for my friend to be abused by her pastor, for example. Yet somehow He has been faithfully redeeming her pain as she fulfills her newfound calling to advocacy, using her scars not only to bring healing to others, but to dismantle the very systems that caused her harm—saving countless souls from ever experiencing that same evil. Does this offer an explanation for her suffering or excuse the harm that was done to her? Absolutely not. Yet, miraculously, there is still healing and purpose growing from the very places where pain and destruction were sown.

God doesn't send sin, destruction, disease, or death into our lives, but in a profoundly beautiful mystery, He somehow takes even the things meant for our harm and uses them for good—the ultimate example of swords turned into plowshares. The key to experiencing this redemptive power is to turn our pain outward, converting our laments of "Why me, God?" into prayers of "Use me, God." This is in no way a justification of our suffering, or a way to condone very real harm done to victims of abuse or injustice, but rather a pathway to find healing through this glorious redemption of our pain.

I love the way Dr. Rob Reimer wrestled with this same enigmatic truth in his book *Soul Care*. He wrote, "It is important for us to believe that God can redeem the pain in our life. Not that God sent it, but that God can redeem it. He turns the arrows of the enemy meant to destroy us into the scalpels of the Great Physician meant to heal us. It gives us hope in every circumstance."[3]

My prayer for you is that you will see your swords turned to plowshares, your deepest hurts converted into a springboard to your greatest calling. The same God who willingly experienced the suffering of humanity to connect with us inside our pain is the God who now faithfully promises to redeem it for our good. Just as our suffering bonds us ever more deeply to Christ, we are now offered the chance to bond more deeply with one another and to create more meaningful community through both comfort and pain. And as our suffering shapes us more and more like the perfect image of Christ, may we follow faithfully in the footsteps of the One who was broken for our benefit and whose wounds became the tools for our healing.

> He has borne our griefs and carried our sorrows; yet we esteemed him stricken, smitten by God, and afflicted. But he was pierced for our transgressions; he was crushed for our iniquities; upon him was the chastisement that brought us peace, *and with his wounds we are healed* (Isaiah 53:4-5, emphasis added).

Don't miss that last phrase. It's the very same one we saw in chapter 2, only in that context we saw it weaponized to tell Christians struggling through disease or disability that their suffering is ultimately in vain, and they lack only the proper faith to be healed. How fitting to end this chapter with one final sword turned plowshare, seeing the very words once used for harm now transfigured by this deepened theology of suffering into the promise of a healing far more glorious than simple deliverance from the common cold.

"He has borne our griefs and carried our sorrows," not only making a way to meet us inside our pain, but also bringing us the very tools for our redemption—"with his wounds we are healed." And if we truly believe the promises we studied back in chapter 5, that our own suffering embodies Christ more fully in us and empowers us to become more like Him (Philippians 3:10; 2 Corinthians 4:8-10)? This means *our* wounds can be transformed into tools of healing and redemption as well.

Chapter 8

Declaration of Interdependence

We might impress people with our strengths, but we
connect with people through our weaknesses.

Craig Groeschel[1]

Years ago, a well-meaning friend gifted us with an educational course from a popular Christian finance guru. Desperate to free us from years of financial struggle, I did my very best to work through all the materials in order to learn the methods.

No matter what your personal financial situation is, this multi-step program has something for you. If you are deeply in debt, you start at the bottom and work on that first. If you are debt-free but still have a home mortgage, you take dramatic steps to pay off your home. Even after your home is paid off, there are still various tasks to complete, all designed to give you even greater financial security and personal wealth.

As a Christian program, the overarching theme of these goals isn't framed in terms of greed, but rather as a desire to reach a place of true independence and self-sufficiency, allowing you to provide generously not only for your own family, but for others as well.

The incredible popularity of this particular financial program does not surprise me. We all desire greater security, and almost no one enjoys the feeling of being dependent on others to meet their needs. "It is more blessed to give than to receive" (Acts 20:35), we quote, and we would prefer to be the people funding charitable causes rather than the ones standing in line for their services. Generosity is a virtue we are called to cultivate intentionally in our own lives and to honor when we recognize it in others. We applaud the philanthropy of folks like Bill Gates. We share viral stories of the football star who takes his newfound wealth and buys a home for his aging mother. We rename hospital wings after their most generous donors.

It's not just about financial generosity either. Churches celebrate those who bring meals to the sick, who visit the elderly in nursing homes, who provide babysitting for the single mother so she can go back to school. We recognize that generosity is a spiritual discipline, so naturally we seek to be givers, rather than takers.

It makes sense, then, that for most of my life I thought of the biblical idea of "the poor" in terms of how we should care for them, and how caring for the poor would serve as a witness for the gospel to an onlooking world. So, when my body was gradually overtaken more and more by Lyme, and I could no longer work a traditional job or even manage my own care without assistance, I was determined to somehow push my way through the barriers and seek self-sufficiency in any way I could. I refused to classify myself as disabled, and whenever I had even a bit of energy I ran myself ragged trying to make up for all the times I wasn't functional.

When I was eventually placed on three months of mandatory bed rest while pregnant with Jack, I had little choice but to accept the generous offers of meals and babysitting for Aidan. However, I regularly assured myself that this was only temporary, and once I was back on my feet I would not only return each and every one of these favors, but I would also pay it forward as well. When the crippling costs of my medical care consistently pulled my family under again and again, despite so many years of sacrifices to try to manage them on our own, I was overcome by a deep sense of guilt and spiritual failure. What I had always believed to be temporary seasons of need had somehow developed into a long-term pattern, with seemingly no hope of us reasonably becoming truly self-sufficient ever again.

I believed in who Christ was and the power of His saving grace, and I earnestly desired to serve God faithfully, but I just could not see how my life was in any way a reflection of those beliefs. I often wondered how I could even consider myself a member of my church anymore, as my declining health meant my attendance was getting abysmal, I almost never signed up to provide snacks for our Sunday-school class or volunteered to serve in the church nursery, and I always seemed to be in some kind of need. I found myself haunted daily by the reminder that "faith apart from works is dead" (James 2:26).

Between my disabilities and our financial struggles, I had lost my place among the givers. I had become a taker. It felt like there just wasn't a place for someone so weak, broken, and suffering to serve God. I wasn't the one ministering to the poor; I *was* the poor, something for which I was deeply ashamed. I pleaded with God for years to heal my body and fix our financial insecurity, convinced that if we could just stand on our own two feet, I could once again find my place in the body of Christ.

You might remember that the quote "Faith apart from works is dead" comes from the second chapter of James. You may also remember when we discussed how the book of James is written in the style of a Jewish wisdom text, focused predominantly on how our inward beliefs translate into outwardly visible behaviors. We actually looked at how this particular teaching comes directly in the context of giving to the poor: "If a brother or sister is poorly clothed and lacking in daily food, and one of you says to them, 'Go in peace, be warmed and filled,' without giving them the things needed for the body, what good is that? *So also faith by itself, if it does not have works, is dead*" (James 2:15-17, emphasis added).

But it's the first half of this very same chapter that began to challenge everything I thought I knew about giving, self-sufficiency, and ultimately about the poor. Let's look at the first four verses to set the stage:

> My brothers, show no partiality as you hold the faith in our Lord Jesus Christ, the Lord of glory. For if a man wearing a gold ring and fine clothing comes into your assembly, and a poor man in shabby clothing also comes in, and if you pay attention to the one who wears the fine clothing and say, "You sit here in a good place," while you say to the poor man, "You stand over there," or, "Sit down at my feet," have you not then made distinctions among yourselves and become judges with evil thoughts? (James 2:1-4).

The idea seems simple enough: The church should not treat the poor any differently than the rich or seek the presence of the powerful any more than the presence of those who are marginalized. At face value, there isn't anything all that radical about what James says. You could draw the natural conclusion from these words that in Christ the rich and the poor are all viewed as equals, and that in the economy of the kingdom of God everyone will ultimately receive the same portion. Yet verse 5 takes a very different turn: "Listen, my beloved brothers, has not God chosen those who are poor in the world to be rich in faith and heirs of the kingdom, which he has promised to those who love him?"

It's a verse that feels downright disruptive and makes me entirely uncomfortable. Just as James cautions us against partiality and making "distinctions among yourselves" (verse 4), he seems to suggest that God is not bound by this same impartiality, that He not only recognizes distinction between the rich and the poor, but that He has *chosen* the poor for special blessing.

Much of Christian tradition in the West tends to embrace the idea that when God one day eliminates all injustice, inequality, and poverty, those who are suffering will be restored to the same joy as those who have plenty. And yet James seems to suggest something different here, a more radical idea that directly echoes the teachings of Christ himself.

When we discussed the beatitudes earlier in chapter 3, I referred to the most commonly read version from the book of Matthew. But did you know there's another version in the book of Luke, a version that contains not only a list of those who are "blessed," but also a list of "woe"?

> Blessed are you who are poor, for yours is the kingdom of God. Blessed are you who are hungry now, for you shall be satisfied. Blessed are you who weep now, for you shall laugh. Blessed are you when people hate you and when they exclude you and revile you and spurn your name as evil, on account of the Son of Man! Rejoice in that day, and leap for joy, for behold, your reward is great in heaven; for so their fathers did to the prophets. But *woe to you who are rich*, for you have received your consolation. *Woe to you who are full now*, for you shall be hungry. *Woe to you who laugh now*, for you shall mourn and weep. *Woe to you, when all people speak well of you*, for so their fathers did to the false prophets (Luke 6:20-26, emphasis added).

This concept is difficult to wrestle with because it's so fundamentally different from much of mainstream theology. As the white American church has grown in affluence and privilege, we've not only given way to the influence of prosperity-gospel teachings that disconnects us from a healthy theology of suffering, but we've also distanced ourselves from the radical, upside-down economics of the kingdom of God. Over time, white churches have predominantly adopted a more accommodating view that focuses only on the hope for the poor and needy, neglecting any mention of Christ's warnings to the privileged. Black American Christians, however, have faced a long and arduous history of struggle and abuse, a painful crucible that has produced a rich theology of suffering with great depth and complexity. I love the way theologian James Cone explains this in his book *The Cross and the Lynching Tree*:

> The cross is the most empowering symbol of God's loving solidarity with the "least of these," the unwanted in society who suffer daily from great injustices. Christians must face the cross as the terrible tragedy it was and discover in it, through faith and repentance, the liberating joy of eternal salvation. But we cannot find liberating joy in the cross by spiritualizing it, by taking away its message of justice in the midst of powerlessness, suffering, and death. The cross, as a locus of divine revelation, is not good news for the powerful, for those who are comfortable with the way things are, or for anyone whose understanding of religion is aligned with power.[2]

The economics of God's kingdom are not simply about restoring equality, but about the reversal of everything we know here on earth. The first will be last; the last will be first; the servants will be the greatest; the weak will be strong; and the poor will be the richest among us. The good news of the gospel is even better news for the poor, the marginalized, and the suffering.

When we embrace this view of the kingdom, it forces us to confront difficult questions about some of our most closely held ideals. Take the example of that popular Christian financial program: If we desire to give more generously to others and provide for the needs of the poor, isn't it only logical that we need to ensure our own financial security and independence first? Can't God bless Christians with the gift of wealth in order to equip them to best serve the kingdom? Shouldn't we strive to be givers and not takers? Yet how can any of this be reconciled with Christ teaching, "Blessed are you who are poor," and, "Woe to you who are rich" (Luke 6:20,24)?

·······························

The economics of God's kingdom are not simply about restoring equality, but about the reversal of everything we know here on earth.

·······························

An Illusion of Independence

I want to return to a letter we've visited a number of times throughout this book, 2 Corinthians, because I think it is in this same letter that we can begin to take these seemingly contradictory ideas and start to piece together a new understanding of how they all come together. I love seeing our themes and passages crossing and intersecting yet again, tying each new revelation together into a deeper, more robust theology of suffering.

> We want you to know, brothers, about the grace of God that has been given among the churches of Macedonia,

for in a severe test of affliction, their abundance of joy
and their extreme poverty have overflowed in a wealth of
generosity on their part. For they gave according to their
means, as I can testify, and beyond their means, of their
own accord, begging us earnestly for the favor of taking
part in the relief of the saints...For you know the grace
of our Lord Jesus Christ, that though he was rich, yet
for your sake he became poor, so that you by his poverty
might become rich...I do not mean that others should
be eased and you burdened, but that as a matter of fairness your abundance at the present time should supply
their need, so that their abundance may supply your
need, that there may be fairness. As it is written, "Whoever gathered much had nothing left over, and whoever
gathered little had no lack" (8:1-4,9,13-15).

Paul writes in praise of the churches in Macedonia, speaking to
this same theme of showing financial generosity. But in a surprising turn, he explicitly informs his readers that these are not believers who carefully stewarded financial abundance for the good of the
kingdom; these are churches in extreme poverty, ones he says gave
not only according to their means but *beyond* their means.

Paul continues by pointing to the example of Christ, in that He
willingly gave up the glory of heaven to take on the form of a man
and come to us here on earth, giving us a chance to experience God's
riches at great cost to Himself. Paul then speaks directly to his readers in Corinth, urging them to follow in the example of giving generously. He makes a point here of explaining that generosity means
giving according to what a person has, not according to what he
does not have. This is important, because it keeps us from seeing
generosity in terms of who gives more than whom, and reminds us

that, ultimately, we are only called to be faithful with what we've been given—no more, no less.

What is really illuminating, though, is what Paul says in those final verses, as he walks us through a blueprint of God's greater design for the body of Christ as a whole. When we view the ideas we've just discussed in terms of individuals or even individual churches, it's easy to feel resistance to the suggestion that we may be called to give of ourselves so generously that we end up needy and poor. It sounds downright illogical, really. When Paul pulls us back to the big-picture view, however, the pieces begin to fall into place.

He tells the believers in Corinth that this call to generosity is not so "others should be eased and you burdened" (verse 13), but so the body of Christ is tied together in a community of interdependence—one where no one is left burdened, because each is being faithfully cared for by the other. "As it is written, 'Whoever gathered much had nothing left over, and whoever gathered little had no lack'" (verse 15). Much like the shiva traditions we discussed in the previous chapter, Paul paints a picture of believers who belong so wholly to one another, intertwined in this cycle of both giving and receiving, that they are fused into a single, unified body.

We can see this same principle echoed in the book of Acts, the earliest framework for what the community of Christ should be.

> They devoted themselves to the apostles' teaching and the fellowship, to the breaking of bread and the prayers. And awe came upon every soul, and many wonders and signs were being done through the apostles. And all who believed were together and had all things in common. And they were selling their possessions and belongings and distributing the proceeds to all, as any had need (Acts 2:42-45).

Now the full number of those who believed were of one heart and soul, and no one said that any of the things that belonged to him was his own, but they had everything in common. And with great power the apostles were giving their testimony to the resurrection of the Lord Jesus, and great grace was upon them all. There was not a needy person among them, for as many as were owners of lands or houses sold them and brought the proceeds of what was sold and laid it at the apostles' feet, and it was distributed to each as any had need (4:32-35).

It is this idea of interdependence that provides the key to putting it all together. How can we be called to cultivate a spirit of generosity while also believing Jesus when He says, "Woe to you who are rich" (Luke 6:24)? How can we faithfully hold that "faith apart from works is dead" (James 2:26) in tension with the belief that God's "grace is sufficient for you, for [His] power is made perfect in weakness" (2 Corinthians 12:9)? How can we seek to be givers when the upside-down economics of Jesus seem to elevate the ones who receive? By recognizing that God's perfect design is that we would all fill both roles.

The body of Christ was never meant to be divided into givers and takers at all, because each member is meant to have "everything in common" and "no one [is meant to say] that any of the things that belonged to him was his own" (Acts 4:32). Each one of us is given opportunities not only to learn the spiritual discipline of giving, but also to strengthen the very real discipline of learning how to humble ourselves in order to receive as well. The goal for the Christian was never meant to be independence and self-sufficiency, but interdependence and sufficiency found only in Christ and shared wholly with one another in community.

One of the unique gifts of suffering is that it so often shatters the illusion of independence that keeps us from experiencing this greater belonging in the body of Christ. For example, life as a woman with disabilities has given me a very different perspective on the idea of "earning" anything in this life. The basic concept that people can earn financial security through hard work and wise choices sounds so different when you're given a body that's physically unable to work, a body that also brings medical bills that outpace most people's mortgages. How exactly do people earn a body that's healthy and free of disability?

Once this curtain is pulled back, a whole slew of similar realizations can be found behind it. How does someone "earn" being born in a wealthy nation with a chance at an education instead of being born into a life of hardship in an economically depressed country? How does someone "earn" being properly loved and nurtured in their childhood instead of neglected or abused, permanently altering their brain for life? How does someone "earn" being born into privilege and opportunity instead of being born into generational poverty? The belief that we have earned anything in this life ultimately hinges on ignoring just how much we are impacted by variables entirely outside our control.

The apostle Paul understood this well:

> *We have this treasure in jars of clay, to show that the surpassing power belongs to God and not to us.* We are afflicted in every way, but not crushed; perplexed, but not driven to despair; persecuted, but not forsaken; struck down, but not destroyed; always carrying in the body the death of Jesus, so that the life of Jesus may also be manifested in our bodies (2 Corinthians 4:7-10, emphasis added).

Notice how that phrase "belongs to God and not to us" sounds like the words from Acts: "No one said that any of the things that belonged to him was his own" (4:32). Paul recognizes that forsaking the framework of "who earned what" is not only about financial wealth or material possessions. Following Christ means giving up the illusion of self-sufficiency in *every* area of life, choosing instead to embrace our identity as empty vessels of clay. It means laying down any pride in our own accomplishments and recognizing them only as evidence of the power of God at work in our life. It means no longer seeing generosity as giving our own resources to others, but as an invitation to experience what God is doing as a mere conduit through which His goodness is channeled. It means forsaking independence as a virtue, choosing instead to admit our complete dependence on God while also seeking to live in vulnerable interdependence with one another.

Consider for a moment that God Himself—the embodiment of complete perfection, strength, and omnipotence—exists in a triune form. In the Trinity, we have a God who dwells in community in and unto Himself, a God in three persons and yet one in perfect unity. As we were created in the image of that God, it seems problematic to think independence could be an element of that design. How could we reflect a perfect state of community if we are meant to seek self-sufficiency and avoid dependence on one another?

God put it plainly with His Genesis pronouncement, "It is not good that the man should be alone" (2:18). We were designed for community. We were not made to be independent, but to experience the deep bonds of interdependence in a truly unified body of Christ. Authentic community is never formed by unidirectional relationships, though, so it is not enough to simply give to others around us. We must embrace the equal importance of learning how to receive and how to share our needs, our weaknesses, and our burdens as well. As Paul puts it, "Bear one another's burdens, and so fulfill the law of Christ" (Galatians 6:2).

We were
designed for
community. We
were not made to
be independent,
but to experience
the deep bonds of
interdependence
in a truly unified
body of Christ.

Unity Through Diversity

It is our suffering and our weaknesses that provide a unique opportunity for the church to "fulfill the law of Christ." Yet there is simply no way for us to "bear one another's burdens" if we are each determined to carry them alone. When we view ourselves in a false hierarchy of the "generous/givers" over the "poor/receivers," we miss the crucial truth that both of these roles are equally necessary for a healthy and functioning body of Christ. We know how to celebrate the woman who serves in the church nursery for so many years, but what about the single mom who consistently asks for free babysitting? We know how to celebrate the person who leads the prayer team, but what about the one who always seems to come forward after the service, tearfully asking time and again for prayer and encouragement? We know how to celebrate the testimonies of change, the success stories of lives transformed by the power of Christ, but what about the present-tense testimonies bravely offered in addiction meetings or accountability groups? Can we see the beauty in the balance, the unity found only in the diversity of our different roles?

When Paul speaks of the church as a body, he says:

> If all were a single member, where would the body be? As it is, there are many parts, yet one body. The eye cannot say to the hand, "I have no need of you," nor again the head to the feet, "I have no need of you." On the contrary, the parts of the body that seem to be weaker are indispensable, and on those parts of the body that we think less honorable we bestow the greater honor, and our unpresentable parts are treated with greater modesty, which our more presentable parts do not require. But God has so composed the body, giving greater honor

to the part that lacked it, that there may be no division in the body, but that the members may have the same care for one another. If one member suffers, all suffer together; if one member is honored, all rejoice together (1 Corinthians 12:19-26).

Paul doesn't ask the Corinthians to downplay or eliminate their differences. No, Paul calls them to unity specifically by highlighting their differences, and then celebrating that very diversity as the key to God's design for the body. Notice how he does not tell them, "Honor the eye for all the good work it is doing, and pray that the hands can one day become more like the eye." He also doesn't say, "The hands have digits, and the feet have digits too! See how similar we all really are in the end? Let's focus only on what we have in common for the sake of unity in the body." Most importantly, he doesn't call them simply to tolerate these differences as an act of grace. He pushes them to recognize their differences as vitally important to God's design, reminding them, "If all were a single member, where would the body be?" (verse 19). And yet Paul knows that inviting us to embrace our differences is not enough, because humans always tend to create hierarchies based on differences. If there must be different roles to play, then which ones are better and which ones are worse? Paul addresses this issue right away; but in another example of the radical upside-down economics of the kingdom, he doesn't simply tell us that all roles are equal. He says that "the parts of the body that seem to be weaker are *indispensable*," and that "on those parts of the body that we think less honorable we bestow the *greater honor*" (verses 22-23, emphasis added).

Remember, Paul is writing this in a letter of pastoral guidance to a real, functioning church, so try to consider for a moment the practical implications these words could have in a church today.

Imagine your pastor introducing a member who is chronically ill and disabled, cannot afford to tithe much of anything, is unable to serve in any volunteer positions, and relies heavily on the benevolence fund to keep up on her medical bills and living expenses. Picture your pastor lovingly wrapping his arm around this woman as he says, "She is absolutely *indispensable* to this church. We just couldn't be whole without her."

Now, imagine your church hosting a yearly awards dinner for members upon whom they wish to *bestow greater honor*. This year's recipients include the man who confessed a struggle with pornography to his men's group, the new members of the addiction support meetings, the woman who left the worship team because she needed to focus on treating her depression, the family that accepted the most financial aid from the benevolence fund this year, and the man with developmental disabilities who is always yelling out distracting words during the time of worship. Does that all sound pretty far fetched? And yet Paul offers a picture that is exactly this radical. He points to the suffering, the weak, the poor, the hurting, the broken, those with disabilities, and the ones who just can't seem to get it right, and he's saying these *indispensable* beloveds are the very keys to making this body of Christ work.

Paul explicitly elevates the marginalized, but why? He explains when he says that "God has so composed the body, giving greater honor to the part that lacked it, *that there may be no division in the body, but that the members may have the same care for one another*" (verses 24-25, emphasis added). Did you catch that? God designed the body of Christ to honor the weak and elevate the position of the marginalized, because that is what ultimately eliminates our earthly divisions, so that "the members may have the same care for one another." Seeing the value of the strong and the accomplished comes instinctually, but it takes intentional cultivation to learn to see that same value in the weak and the marginalized.

When we see ourselves as the givers, and the needy members of our church as recipients of our generosity, there is division. But when we learn to elevate the needy and to actively see them as invaluable members of this body, whom we need even more greatly than they need us? Then we build authentic two-way relationships, wherein each member is able both to give and to receive, and the body is strengthened by the bonds of our interdependence. That interdependence in turn creates the truest form of unity, in which "if one member suffers, all suffer together; if one member is honored, all rejoice together" (verse 26).

How can we move the church toward this greater unity and interdependence? It requires each of us to make a commitment to radical authenticity. This is a biblical authenticity that shares our weaknesses just as openly as our victories. It's recognizing that if His strength is truly made perfect in our weakness, then pedestals are just stumbling blocks and platforms are just greater heights from which we can fall.

There was a time recently when I realized I was still struggling to consistently apply a particular truth I was tasked with teaching. I found myself saying, "I have no business sharing these insights right now! How can I be teaching anyone if I'm still messing up on this?" I had to swallow a heaping portion of humility in order to recognize my pure hubris in thinking there would *ever* come a time in this life when I have *any* sacred truths perfectly mastered. I realized there was an unholy desire in myself to be seen as "the giver" again—this time as the giver of knowledge, the one who teaches "those other people, the ones who just don't get it like I do." Radical authenticity is admitting that, for all the truths I've shared in this book, I'm still preaching them to my own heart as much as I'm preaching them to yours. It means owning my weaknesses instead of creating false divisions between myself and my readers. I'm reminded of another piece in 1 Corinthians, where Paul says:

> I, when I came to you, brothers, did not come proclaiming to you the testimony of God with lofty speech or wisdom. For I decided to know nothing among you except Jesus Christ and him crucified. And I was with you in weakness and in fear and much trembling, and my speech and my message were not in plausible words of wisdom, but in demonstration of the Spirit and of power, so that your faith might not rest in the wisdom of men but in the power of God (2:1-5).

Biblical authenticity isn't only about exposing our weaknesses. It is also about a willingness to play whatever role we have been given, to embrace our identity as an image bearer of God, and to seek to reflect that image accurately, without edits or filters.

When Aidan was about six years old, he prayed a heartbreaking bedtime prayer asking God to "please take away my autism so I can just be like everyone else." No matter how much we tried to speak positively of his autism, he had become painfully aware that he was different from the other kids in many ways.

I told Aidan that being made in God's image means that we have a God who's so big and so multifaceted that it takes each and every one of us to carry all these difference pieces of His huge reflection. It takes men; it takes women. It takes all our different races and cultures. It takes our different strengths and abilities, all our various personality traits and quirks, and all sorts of subtle ways we see and interact with the world differently, all to piece together the fullest possible picture of this complex God we reflect. I told Aidan that his

autism is a vital piece of showing us different aspects of God's character, things we may not have caught a glimpse of if he was "just like
everyone else." I said that he was given an important role, a role only
he is uniquely qualified to play; so if he doesn't play his special part,
we will all lose that vital piece of who God is, forever hidden from
our view. The apostle Paul puts it this way: "Only let each person
lead the life that the Lord has assigned to him, and to which God has
called him. This is my rule in all the churches" (1 Corinthians 7:17).

The context of the verse comes as Paul is settling a dispute in the
churches about circumcision. Some were saying that Gentiles who
wanted to follow Christ should be circumcised as the Jews had been.
It was a regular source of debate, and ultimately boiled down to various factions of the church who felt they were the ones that should
be emulated, and other Christians should seek to be more like them.
Paul sets them straight with a clear edict that those who are already
circumcised should stay that way. Those who are not? Well, they
should stay that way too. He tells the believers in no uncertain terms,
"Only let each person lead the life that the Lord has assigned to him,
and to which God has called him." It is a call to biblical authenticity, to embrace whatever role we've been given to play and to recognize the holy calling God has placed on our life to display a unique
facet of His image.

Walter Brueggemann once said, "I think it's more important for
the church to be the most honest place in town, than it is for the
church to be the happiest place in town."[3] Imagine a church filled
with this kind of radical authenticity, where suffering and weakness
are shared as equally as victories and strengths. Imagine a church
where each member embraces their unique callings, and where every
role is seen as a sacred duty to accurately reflect the image of God.
Imagine a church where the weak and needy are valued as utterly
indispensable, and where the strong see only the power of God at

work through them as empty vessels. Imagine a church where every member shares not only their resources but also their needs, so that each member gets the holy opportunity to bear up the burdens of another—and so fulfill the law of Christ.

This is what a church with a healthy theology of suffering can be, a church that truly becomes the most honest—and most connected—place in town.

Chapter 9

Blessed Are the Reckless

Hope is that thing inside us that insists, despite all the evidence
to the contrary, that something better awaits us if we have the
courage to reach for it, and to work for it, and to fight for it.

BARACK OBAMA[1]

Growing up in a conservative Baptist tradition, there wasn't a lot of focus on the Holy Spirit in the church I attended. The Spirit was all but synonymous with your conscience, a divine Jiminy Cricket who urges people to avoid sin and choose the right. I was raised to be wary of more charismatic traditions of faith, skeptical of those who claimed to speak in tongues or prophesy at the Spirit's urging. Prayer was always directed to the Father (God, our heavenly Father, our Father in heaven) or to the Son (Jesus, Christ, Savior, etc.). I remember experiencing such jarring discomfort the first time I heard someone open a prayer addressing the "beautiful Holy Spirit"; it was as if he had just prayed to the Ghost of Christmas Past.

I often joke that our real Trinity was the Father, Son, and Holy Bible. Scripture was seen as the only true way to determine God's guidance, and the idea of people "feeling" the Spirit was often met with the rebuke that "the heart is deceitful above all things, and desperately sick; who can understand it?" (Jeremiah 17:9).

A couple years ago, my family and I found ourselves attending a new church in a denomination with which I was somewhat unfamiliar—the Christian and Missionary Alliance. The founder of the denomination came from the Presbyterian tradition, but in the late nineteenth century, he was deeply influenced by the Holiness movement and the more charismatic elements of Christian faith. Alliance churches adopt a statement of theology they call the "Fourfold Gospel": four central truths about who Jesus is that shape the foundations for how Alliance churches practice the liturgies of faith. Each of these four aspects are represented by an icon, and those four icons make up the symbolic logo of the denomination. Christ the Savior is represented by the cross. Christ the Sanctifier is represented by a laver—an image resembling a cup, which serves as a depiction of the basin in the Hebrew tabernacle for washing hands and feet before entering the holy presence of God. Christ the Coming King is represented by a crown, a reminder of the return of Christ to reign over His kingdom. The fourth icon is a pitcher, representing oil to anoint the sick and the unwavering belief in Christ the Healer.

When we first joined an Alliance church, I was unaware of the central nature this commitment to healing plays in the denomination—and in this local church specifically. The topic of faith healings was something I had written about at length, and none of it was positive. In examining the prosperity gospel and the implications of a theology of suffering, I had seen countless examples of faith healing approached in wholly unbiblical ways. I had also experienced great personal wounding in this area.

There were those who suggested God would only heal my disabilities if I had a pure enough faith. Or they claimed that my lack of healing could suggest an area of hidden sin in my life, which my continuing pain was meant to call into repentance. There was the church that made wildly inappropriate disabled parking signs that featured the symbol of a person in a wheelchair with the phrase "Soon to be healed." There was the woman who told me she was praying for Aidan to be healed of "the curse of autism," and I could "take hope in knowing there would be no more autism in heaven"— which was all problematic enough without her saying this right in front of Aidan himself. Yes, faith healing and I had a painful history to say the least, and we were no longer on speaking terms.

Turn back for a moment to the beginning of chapter 2, where we started working through this theology of suffering together. Do you see how we began with this very same theme, a conversation on faith healing handled in all the wrong ways? We've spent seven chapters peeling back the lies of the prosperity gospel and rebuking both the influences of triumphalism and facades of false optimism. And yet all throughout this book we keep returning to one familiar theme: the sacred balance in tension, the perfect truths found in seeming contradiction. For all the ways we have grappled with those conflicts, there is still a larger, more difficult tension that encircles it all, forcing us to take our newfound understanding and surrender it in a place of mystery and dissonance once again. It is a truth with which I have spent the last two years wrestling. This chapter is an outpouring of a lesson I'm still learning in the present, a truth I've become convicted is simply too vital to the theology of suffering to leave unsaid.

Just because God never promised us a miracle baby, an anonymous check to magically cover all our expenses, or instant physical healing on this side of eternity, that doesn't mean I'm not still called to ask for them, again and again. It doesn't mean I shouldn't humble myself into what feels like outright naivete and choose the terrifying vulnerability of believing He just might do it—all while submitting myself wholly to His will and the acceptance that He may say no once again.

When I agreed to write this book, I was only weeks away from starting treatment for my newly diagnosed Lyme disease. The therapies were very expensive and not at all covered by insurance, and so my family had spent months trying to raise as much support as we could. Ultimately, we fell very short of the goal, and I faced the excruciating possibility of having to delay treatment until the specialist's next potential opening—a full six months later.

I was the sickest I had ever been. Crippled by fatigue, I spent an average of four days a week mostly confined to bed. My short-term memory was almost entirely inaccessible, and my speaking abilities had been replaced by nearly insurmountable aphasia. (Aphasia is a condition of the brain where you lose the ability to communicate. You understand what it is you are trying to say, but the actual words themselves are missing, like pages deleted from a dictionary. It's like trying to use your high-school French to order dinner, but you just can't remember the word for *chicken*.) I had regular seizures; my degenerative arthritis was so advanced that I required a cane for mobility much of the time; and my dominant hand was plagued by a persistently recurring tremor.

But with a publishing deal came an advance that was enough to cover—almost exactly—the costs of my first rounds of treatment and my travel to and from the out-of-state clinic. When I held the check in my hand, I marveled at how God had shown up in my most painful place and used that very pain to deliver me a miracle. At the same time, I began to quietly give foothold in my mind to this idea that now, after 15 years of pain and disease, I was finally "ready" to be healed. I had learned the lessons He wanted me to understand so that this book could become the testimony of all I had discovered from that long season of suffering. It was finally time to come into a new season of rest and reward.

Are you seeing the irony, my friend? Once again we find ourselves circling back to the start. Remember our first chapter, the story of my unmet expectations and my deep misunderstanding of the ongoing brokenness inherent in this human experience? What's even more ironic is that that was the very chapter I had just finished writing. I had quite literally just walked through the memories of how badly I had gotten this wrong in the past, and yet there I was again, giving myself over to the hidden roots of prosperity thinking.

When the treatments ended up giving me only moderate improvement from certain symptoms and not a total healing from Lyme, I was devastated—but that wasn't the only disappointment I would face. Just as I was scheduled to begin writing, my family suffered a series of catastrophic financial blows that meant we'd likely lose the incredible home that brought us to Oregon in the first place. I was reliving the crushing roller-coaster ride of chapter 1 all over again.

A crazy plan came together that could potentially provide a last-ditch effort to refinance our mortgage and save our home, but it would mean spending the next four months focused singularly on a huge list of home improvement projects, most of them requiring a lot of physical labor on my part. The book would have to be delayed. For those next four months, I threw myself into trying to keep my family's heads above the waterline, believing once again that if I could just get to that next benchmark, I would finally be able to settle in to a season of calm and write this book in peace.

I'm guessing you won't be surprised to read that exactly nothing went according to plan, and the four months of carefully planned projects became nine months of sheer chaos. We came incredibly close to losing everything at least half a dozen separate times, and we were always hard pressed under the reality that we balanced precariously on a razor's edge. At one point in the process I suffered what can only be described as a nervous breakdown, and I was eventually diagnosed with complex post-traumatic stress disorder (C-PTSD). So many years of ongoing pain, loss, illness, insecurity, and trauma had taken their toll on my body and mind. I wasn't sleeping; I would go for days with hardly eating; and I was having panic attacks on a near daily basis.

I would be lying if I didn't tell you I strongly considered walking away from writing at that point, as I was desperately longing for a chance to catch my breath and choose a season of prioritizing only healing and self-care. This book had been the culmination of a life-long dream, and yet suddenly it felt like a weight tied to my ankle as I desperately thrashed in my attempts to tread water.

Losing Control

I don't remember exactly how it happened, because so much of this season is a blur, but in the midst of this place of broken-ness I found myself sitting in my first-ever Pentecost service. I was still pretty new to our Alliance church because our chaotic circum-stances had left our attendance pretty abysmal in that first year. I remember feeling anxious and uncertain, because a special service that focused entirely on the power of the Holy Spirit felt like some kind of unnatural mysticism to me. I was deeply skeptical, and yet there was a part of me that craved something more, longing for a faith that held bigger things than what I could explain or even hope to understand. I had met Jesus so intimately back on that bathroom floor, but the Holy Spirit remained a distant acquaintance.

At a certain point in the service I heard a song that was new to me about the Holy Spirit causing change in our perspective and motivation called "Spirit of the Living God." I don't have an expla-nation for what happened next. For most of my life I would have read the following with a deep sense of skepticism, likely rolling my eyes. Sitting there alone on the far side of my pew, I heard a distinctly audible voice calling me by name and quietly urging me to open my Bible to Romans 8. It's a chapter we've seen before in this book, about how God redeems even the most painful circumstances for our good (verse 28), and how nothing can ultimately separate us from Him (verses 37-39). On this night, though, my eyes went somewhere else entirely, locking in on a passage that felt new and unfamiliar to me. As the crowd around me repeated the song lyrics again and again, I read these words:

> In this hope we were saved. Now hope that is seen is not hope. For who hopes for what he sees? But if we hope for what we do not see, we wait for it with patience. Likewise the Spirit helps us in our weakness. For we do not know what to pray for as we ought, but the Spirit himself intercedes for us with groanings too deep for words. And he who searches hearts knows what is the mind of the Spirit, because the Spirit intercedes for the saints according to the will of God (Romans 8:24-27).

Two key ideas from this passage struck me simultaneously. First, the repeated theme of hope. The word appears five times in the span of two sentences. Ironically, at the time I was participating in a One Little Word campaign where people are encouraged to forgo traditional New Year's resolutions and choose a single word of inspiration instead. My word for the year had actually been *hope*, but I had chosen my word when we had the confident assurance that a cure was finally just over the horizon for me. It was this promise of a cure that had brought the return of hope for the first time in over a decade. But *hope* had been a misnomer, a fact that these verses now brought to my attention. "Now hope that is seen is *not* hope. For who hopes for what he sees?" (verse 24, emphasis added). Hope isn't really hope if you're betting on a sure thing or taking only the most calculated risks with carefully projected outcomes.

I felt a strong resistance to what I was reading, and an even stronger resistance to the response I felt those words were urging: getting up from my seat, heading down the aisle to the prayer team, and praying for healing. I knew beyond a shadow of a doubt that God had never promised I'd be healed this side of eternity. I embraced the idea that God was meeting me in my suffering. I believed that He could turn these painful swords into plowshares. My singular goal was to come to the place I considered true spiritual maturity, a place of total acceptance where I no longer asked God to release me from my earthly struggle.

Yet there it was in black and white: "If we hope for what we do not see, *we wait for it with patience*" (verse 25, emphasis added). Not only was I being urged to ask for the improbable, perhaps even the impossible, but I was being called to "wait for it with patience" as well? This appeared in every way to be an outright contradiction of everything I knew about suffering, squarely in opposition to what I wrote in the past seven chapters. How could I "wait for it with patience" without the false assurance that I could "name and claim" my way to healing, that my miracle was only a matter of "when" and not an undetermined "if"?

The second half of the passage contained equally vexing ideas for me. "We do not know what to pray for as we ought" (verse 26). Well, this part I actually agreed with wholeheartedly. I had even written a blog post at one point about how I was trying a new spiritual discipline where I no longer prayed for any specific requests, asking of God only, "Your will be done." Yet that now felt confusing and in conflict with the very idea of hope as something that requires us to ask for the impossible. The contradictions only multiplied when I realized that I was equally uncomfortable with the notion of a Holy

Spirit who isn't simply trying to guide me, but is actively speaking and interceding on my behalf. The idea suggested that God actually receives those words as if they are my own prayers. I found myself bitterly resistant to the way this seemed to cut me out of my own prayers entirely. I questioned how prayer could be meaningful if it wasn't fully within my own free will to control.

Control. Something about that word grabbed my attention as I continued to wrestle silently with God in my seat, and it completely derailed my train of thought. The voice was no longer audible, but the message was equally clear as I heard it whisper from deep inside me: "You've traded the lie of the prosperity gospel for the comfort of cynicism, blinded to the truth that both are the fruit of the same poisoned tree, the same root sin of control."

Wait...what? How on earth could trying to manipulate God with "name and claim" prayers have anything in common with cynicism? And was it even really fair to label me a cynic? I was simply trying to be a *realist*, recognizing that healing wasn't in the cards for me and striving to come to a place of acceptance. *That's not being negative*, I thought to myself defensively. *That's just being wise.*

I shut my Bible in frustration, without the usual tenderness I tried to give the well-worn mess of pages tucked inside a loose leather cover. Bookmarks and slips of paper came tumbling down onto my lap and all across the ground around my feet. Annoyed, I began to tuck each little scrap in the front cover so I could reorganize them another time. My eyes glanced across the final item as I laid it on the stack, a handwritten note card bearing this verse: "Because he bends down to listen, I will pray as long as I have breath!" (Psalm 116:2 NLT).

The card was a vestige of another time, penned before my family made that leap of faith to Oregon only to watch our dreams disintegrate into dust. That was back when I filled stacks of journal pages with prayer requests, coming before the throne again and again to ask for anything and everything in Jesus's holy name. That was back when I shared with anyone who would listen what I was watching for God to do in my life. I hardly recognized the girl I was then. She seemed utterly naive in the way she so publicly chased after the impossible. She was so full of hope.

That was before, I thought to myself, *before I learned how to fully accept my suffering.* Hope seemed so juvenile and unsophisticated to me now, the wide-eyed longings of a girl with her head in the clouds. I didn't need the childish trappings of hope, because I had found endurance instead.

Endurance. Once again, a single word grabbed me, detouring my thoughts to verses I now knew by heart, verses I think you'll recognize: "We rejoice in our sufferings, knowing that suffering produces *endurance*, and endurance produces character, and character produces *hope*" (Romans 5:3-4, emphasis added). *How can this possibly produce hope?* I cried out silently. *This doesn't fit!* I found myself arguing with God, pointing out all the ways this just wasn't right. *Imagine what people would think if I went from preaching this message of sacred lament to some sort of shallow Pinterest gospel of sunshine and rainbows.*

How could God ask me to even consider hope if He also wanted me to finish this book? It would destroy everything I had worked on these past two years, and I would be made a fool. I reopened my Bible, furiously flipping back to Romans, determined to find a more logical answer. Perhaps if I could double-check the context, I'd find some key word or new phrase that could redefine this "hope" to mean something else, something less foolish and risky. I read through verses 3 and 4 of Romans 5 again, and when I reached verse 5 I was taken aback. I had seen this verse so many times throughout the course of my study on suffering, and yet somehow it was like I'd never truly read it before: "*Hope does not put us to shame*, because

God's love has been poured into our hearts through the Holy Spirit who has been given to us" (emphasis added).

"Hope does not put us to shame," the verse says. I had seen hope as only one of two things: either the product of naive ignorance and prosperity theology, or taking the imprudent risk of disappointment and humiliation. This is not the sort of hope that comes from prosperity thinking, though, since Paul so clearly describes it as the product of suffering, endurance, and strong character. So, is it a reckless sort of hope, an ill-advised gamble that's likely to fail? "Hope does not put us to shame," I read again. *But how could it not?* I cried out in my heart. *If I let everyone see me ask for the impossible, and yet come up empty handed, how can that bring anything but shame? Why not just surrender to Your will and wait to see what You decide? Why take the risk of asking for the wrong things?*

The same silent voice repeated the words I had rejected once before. "Stephanie, you've traded the lie of the prosperity gospel for the comfort of cynicism, blinded to the truth that they're the fruit of the same poisoned tree, the same root sin of *control.*" This was followed by the audible voice of a man up on the platform, praying specifically for the Holy Spirit to "remove the scales from our eyes and reveal new truths we've been blinded from understanding."

I began to weep openly in deep, heaving sobs. It was as if these tears were somehow cleansing my eyes to finally see what I had been missing. I had built up so many walls in the name of accepting my suffering, but in truth they were attempts to avoid the very real vulnerability of being asked to submit myself continually to His will. I wanted this faith to be a one-and-done decision, rather than a process of continuing trust. I hadn't stopped asking for healing because I was spiritually mature; I had stopped asking because I was unwilling to risk the disappointment again or to look foolish for thinking it was possible in the first place.

Holy Unease

"Hope does not put us to shame." It was the pivotal missing piece, the cornerstone that allowed the rest of the puzzle to start taking shape at last. God isn't calling us to radical acts of prayer to prove our willingness to be made fools for the sake of obedience. His Word is clear: There is no outcome in which we would be put to shame.

Remember the verses from Romans 8? The Holy Spirit moves in power to speak on our behalf, praying not only the words we lack, but those we simply can't speak. We're offered a picture of prayer with the Trinity operating in perfect unity: the sanctification of the Son bringing us before the throne of our Father who listens, and the Spirit speaking boldly on our behalf. This Romans 8 call to pray for the impossible isn't a test, but rather an invitation to experience God's work in our lives as participants rather than bystanders. Consider Romans 5:5 again: "Hope does not put us to shame, *because God's love has been poured into our hearts through the Holy Spirit who has been given to us*" (emphasis added).

Hope does not put us to shame because God's love has *already* been poured into our hearts, and we have an even greater opportunity to experience that love through the Holy Spirit who has been given to us. In relegating the Spirit to the role of a cartoon angel whispering advice on my shoulder, I had disconnected myself from the fullness of God's power. Hope wasn't the childish unicorn I had imagined; it was the embodiment of God's mighty Spirit in me. I was looking for hope as a cheerful word embroidered brightly across a pillow, when it was a war-battered soldier showing up for yet another fight, outnumbered and outgunned, but still believing she can win. I was looking for hope as an anchor to cling to or as a shelter to huddle in, safe from the raging storm. Now I see hope in the story of Jacob wrestling with God—less as a place of rest and more as a grappling struggle to fight for more of His power and presence.

After all this study of suffering, after this long journey that has unfolded since the stories of chapter 1, I had seemingly come full circle to a place of tension and contradiction once again. I wasn't that same woman who had first come to Oregon, though, because I had learned that truth is never defined by what makes the most sense, and I had seen God most embodied in truths that felt so contradictory. My dear friend and fellow sufferer of chronic illness, Katie Jo Ramsey, put this so perfectly when she wrote, "Cognitive dissonance is the birthplace of all abiding Christian hope. Don't run from what does not make sense. Embrace mystery as the place God dwells."[2] This was as strong a place of cognitive dissonance as I had ever experienced: I still stood firmly against the prosperity gospel and the problematic views of faith healing, and yet I also felt just as strongly that God was calling me to get up from my seat and ask for miraculous healing anyway.

Everything in me wanted to sit frozen in place, but the truth of Romans 8:26 began to play out in that pew: "The Spirit helps us in our weakness. For we do not know what to pray for as we ought, but the Spirit himself intercedes for us." I didn't ask for the strength to stand up from my seat, but my legs began to carry me forward toward the front of the sanctuary. I made a beeline for a somewhat familiar face, and before I could articulate my rationalizations for why I was justified in my skepticism, I found myself pouring out raw and unfiltered confessions instead. I pled guilty to the ways my root desire for security and control had grown into a full-fledged stronghold of cynicism.

My newfound confessor and I spoke for some time, and she was so faithfully attuned to the leadings of the Spirit that she began to ask questions pertaining not only to my physical health, but to a number of hidden traumas and their impact on my mental health as well. I wasn't even considering the idea of healing in this area, so I was pretty taken aback to hear her speak to these things, all without ever knowing my story. And yet, even then my skepticism still gripped me tightly, and I felt painfully aware of how long I had been up front on those steps and how many eyes could be watching this vulnerable display.

I felt uneasy in this space of contradiction. I preferred to choose a side and stand comfortably in certainty. On my left, there was the familiar security of "faithfully accepting" my sickness, a spiritualized cynicism that would happily welcome me back inside its armored walls. On my right, I could see the miracle of healing after so many years of pain. The woman across from me looked straight into my eyes and asked unflinchingly, "Do you believe in the power of Christ the Healer, and would you like to ask for His healing right now?"

It was the final fork in the road, the moment in which I would need to choose how this Pentecost story would end. There was a painfully drawn-out silence as a game of spiritual "chicken" unfolded in the space of that breathless pause. When I finally opened my mouth, I heard the words of a verse I knew so well: "I believe; help my unbelief!" (Mark 9:24).

This was the rallying cry of hope, the perfect truth found in sacred dissonance. I had been so convinced that God required my certainty, and yet I found myself still standing in that place of uncomfortable contradictions. My belief and my unbelief were wound together and laid before a God whose power is made perfect in my weakness, whose grace abounds all the more in the places I am most lacking.

As I sat on those steps, the woman anointed me with oil as she fervently offered prayers of healing over my body and mind until the service ended. I wept as her words washed over me, and I was surprised to find myself offering nods of agreement and even timid echoes of "Yes, Lord, I ask that too." I wasn't just accepting her intercession; I was participating in it. I chose to show up before the throne and admit that yes, I wanted healing. Yes, I wanted to see the end of my Lyme. Yes, I wanted to be free of panic attacks and flashbacks and all the scars of trauma. I wanted the miracle. I wanted to believe. I wanted to fight the fight of hope.

. . . .

My belief and my unbelief were wound together and laid before a God whose power is made perfect in my weakness, whose grace abounds all the more in the places I am most lacking.

. . . .

As I write these words today, I have not yet experienced the miracle of healing.

I want to pause here and let those words linger, to give you a chance to process some of the inevitable responses they inspire. You may be wondering why I would choose to tell you this story if it has such a seemingly unfulfilling ending. Perhaps you're guessing that the surprise moral of this chapter is to double down on criticisms of faith healings after all. Maybe you find yourself asking, "Was it her unbelief that kept her from the miracle, because she needed to have more faith?" You might even be saying, "Maybe the miracle just hasn't come yet; maybe that service put something into motion that just hasn't been completed." I could understand each and every one of these responses. So why did I tell you this story, and what is its lesson?

Friend, I told you this story because I meant what I said in the preface: that this book is a testimony in process, an anthem to a God who's showing up right now inside my painfully broken places. A meaningful theology of suffering cannot be found by swinging the pendulum to the opposite side of the same faulty beliefs. If I lead you into cynicism, then that would be exactly what I've done—swinging the pendulum. And just as I've worked to dismantle the simplistic platitudes of prosperity thinking, I would be equally remiss if I offered an oversimplified theology claiming to have easy answers for our pain.

The most sacred truths are found in the most uncomfortable places, and the theology of suffering can be no exception. We're called to something so much more difficult than the assumption that we fully understand, and thereby accept, our pain. We're called to embrace the holy unease of recognizing that we serve a God beyond our human comprehension, whose ways simply cannot be easily explained by our limited understanding. We're asked to keep questioning, to keep wrestling, to keep coming back to pray for the impossible—even as we acknowledge that we aren't promised the answers in this life. Most importantly, we're asked to remain cognizant of the very real possibility that we're getting some of this wrong, that we don't understand nearly as much as we'd like to think, and that there will inevitably be times that "we do not know what to pray for as we ought" (Romans 8:26).

These challenging and seemingly contradictory truths are the very reason I had the words *immeasurably more* tattooed on my wrist as a permanent reminder. They come from Paul's letter to the Ephesians:

> Now to him who is able to do *immeasurably more* than all we ask or imagine, according to his power that is at work within us (3:20 NIV, emphasis added).

We're asked
to keep questioning,
to keep wrestling,
to keep coming
back to pray for
the impossible —
even as we
acknowledge that
we aren't
promised the
answers in this life.

I will forever love the way this single verse perfectly marries two truths that I've found some of the most challenging to fit together. First, God *is able*, so we should continue to come boldly before the throne with audacious hope. Second, we are told that His ways are ultimately *immeasurably more* than anything we can even *imagine* to ask for—echoing the reminder that "we do not know what to pray for as we ought" (Romans 8:26).

His ways are so far beyond what I can even imagine, let alone hope to understand. Do I know why God asked me to pray so publicly for healing that night? I could list off all the positive outcomes from that experience, but none of them come anywhere close to serving as an explanation for the "why." Do I know if He will choose to heal me in this world, or only with the perfect healing I'll receive in the next? I truly don't. It's a mystery to me even now. But that's the power of my story, the power of hope that abounds from my most broken places and in the face of my greatest disappointments. The fact that I have not received healing should not detract from the message. Rather, it proves these sacred truths to be all the more reliable.

Oh, how mighty the power of a God who can make beauty from ashes and perfect truth from apparent contradictions! I didn't receive a miracle that night, but I still fervently believe that I was called to ask for one. I know God has not promised me physical healing in this life, but I hold equally to the truth that He is able, more than able, to do it anyway. I am held in the loving arms of a God whose faithfulness is not defined by when or if I receive healing, but by His devoted presence in the midst of my deepest pain. I know that neither height, nor depth, nor Lyme, nor miscarriage, nor trauma, nor grief, nor the disappointment of seemingly unanswered prayer, nor anything else in this life can ever separate me from His love.

This I call to mind,
and therefore I have hope:
The steadfast love of the LORD never ceases;
his mercies never come to an end;
they are new every morning;
great is your faithfulness.
"The LORD is my portion," says my soul,
"therefore I will hope in him."

LAMENTATIONS 3:21-24

Acknowledgments

An enormous thank-you to my dearest **Edith Taylor**. Apparently they can't include an acknowledgment comprised entirely of GIFs, so this will have to somehow suffice. I couldn't possibly do my gratitude justice here. You've been more than my best friend—you've been my constant sounding board, my rock, and far and away my most vocal cheerleader. Even Bobby thought your name should be first! You're my Aaron, forever holding up my arms when I'm too weak. You've seen me at my absolute worst, and yet I've never once had to worry I could lose you. You were there in the front row (beaming with pride, I might add) when I first uttered the words *"sacred suffering,"* and when I came down the steps from preaching you said something I'll never forget: "You were born for this. It was like watching a fish put into water." That's who you've always been, though, boldly calling out giftings I don't yet see in myself. You knew this book would exist long before I did—and you still have the photo on your phone to prove it. I couldn't have done any of it without you.

To my husband, **Bobby**, thank you for not being remotely phased that your name came after Edith's. But in all seriousness, you have never been one to seek out thanks. You selflessly ensured I had whatever I needed to reach the finish line, and you never once made me feel guilty for pursuing this calling. Thanks for reminding me that sometimes I do in fact have to eat something. Thanks for always getting up out of bed to get me all the things I'm too lazy to get for myself. Thanks for the way you constantly tell our boys that their mother is "the smart one." But most importantly, thank you for never buying into the idea that I needed to hold my passions for biblical study back in the name of "letting you lead." You've always propelled me only forward, visibly taking pride in seeing me grow into the potential you always knew was there. I will always be grateful for that. I would never have seen this dream come true without you constantly assuring me that I even *could.*

I would be remiss if I didn't acknowledge my two incredible boys, without whom this book would likely have been completed so much sooner. (Yes, Aidan, that was a joke!) *Aidan*, you've taught me more about bravery than anyone I've ever known. Despite all the ways this book required my time and attentions, you stepped up to the plate and showed some of your very best flexible thinking. I'm so grateful for that sacrifice. I'm beyond proud to be your mom. *Jack-Jack*, you bring so much joy and light to our family. Life would be so utterly boring without you. Thanks for giving up so much of mama's attention to let me write. And yes, I still owe you a Target popcorn.

In thinking of the people who made this book possible, I would have to begin with my parents, ***Bill and Doreen Heenk***. You took a three-year-old girl the social workers could only describe as "precocious" and gave her the love and safety to blossom. From dance lessons, to my piano, to the endless art sets, to all the years of private school tuition, you gave me every opportunity to flourish. You nurtured my seemingly boundless mental energy when so many would have understandably looked to confine it, and I owe everything I've become to that choice.

After my parents, there were two women who shaped writing from a young age, **Mrs. Linda Rhone** and **Mrs. Dolores Crouch**. Mrs. Rhone, my mother still tells the story fondly of when you found me at five years old looking up the word "family" in the dictionary and gave her the information for Canterbury. You never stifled my curiosity either, but faithfully planted the seeds in me that ultimately grew into my passion for learning. You also put me directly on the path to Mrs. Crouch. Dolores, you saw a writer in me, and you continually spoke that identity over me until I could finally embrace it for myself. You were responsible for entering not one but two pieces of my writing into contests that year, the first time I ever felt the thrill of seeing my words "published." I still remember fondly all the times I would return to your classroom over the years, bringing journals full of poetry and freshly completed works of fiction, still wanting your feedback most of all. Something tells me you knew this book would exist long before I ever reached adulthood.

There is one person, though, that put this particular book into motion more than anyone else, and that is **Jeff Wetherell**. Jeff was responsible not only for recommending me as a speaker to NCU, where I gave the message that ultimately formed the framework for this book, but he was also the person that reached out to me a year later and asked, "Would you ever considered turning this into a book?" Jeff, I'm so grateful you asked if you could drop my name in front of an editor. I'm also eternally grateful that editor was the incomparable **Kathleen Kerr**. Oh, Kathleen, sometimes I was so afraid you had bitten off more than you expected by taking me on. Between the anxious neuroses of a first-time author and the seemingly never-ending delays that stalled this book, you were a constant ally and tireless supporter. You helped shepherd the most delicate pieces of my shattered heart into something beautifully redeemed. Thank you for taking a risk on me.

There are so many other people worthy of thanks. *Troy Dean*, thanks for taking a chance on a relative unknown when you offered me the opportunity to speak. More than that, thanks for seeing the seeds of something special in that fateful blog post and asking me to consider speaking from that pain. And to *the students at NCU* (there are too many of you to list by name), thanks for the way so many of you embraced me in the earliest days of my work. I felt like a veritable celebrity every time I came on campus.

Kara Brown, without you there would never have been a final chapter. Without you the story would have ended without *hope*. Thanks for speaking boldly to the invisible wounds I hadn't yet been brave enough to admit I was carrying. We can't heal what we won't name.

Andrea, Kaitlyn, Lindsay, Shannon, and Stephanie: Okay, it's official, this group is going to need a name before Shannon has to write out all these names in *her* acknowledgments. But seriously, what an incredible honor it's been to share the sacred space we've somehow created. I sincerely tried not to include any raspberry buzzer-worthy offenses in these pages.

Hannah Brencher, thanks for telling me to get off my behind and do...the...WORK. I knew that you were never going to accept any excuses for giving up, and sometimes that was the only thing that kept me from quitting. I hope what I've created makes you proud.

Shannan Martin and Hayley Morgan, thanks for speaking life over me so many times along the process of this book. It was invaluable having women who were further along in this journey who not only shared their wisdom and experience, but also treated me like I was worthy to be called a friend and peer. I could never fully explain what that has meant to me.

Nish Weiseth, thanks most importantly for *Speak*. I don't know if I would have ever set off down this path if it weren't for that book. Thanks for letting me pick your brain about the industry and for giving generously of your time and wisdom to someone with nothing to offer in return.

Carlos Rodriguez, Jonathan Martin, Major, and Jason Fileta: First and foremost, thanks for going above and beyond that night in Portland to make sure I had a safe place to stay when my tremor made it unsafe to drive. The way you guys showed such genuine brotherly love and concern was like a healing salve for some really deep wounds. Each one of you has spoken encouragement and support into me at various points of this journey, and I have been so grateful to see the ways that each of you use your own platforms to honor and elevate the voices of your sisters in Christ. You're all turning swords into plowshares.

Mike McHargue, thanks for affirming me, validating me, and most importantly, *believing* me. You're one of the good ones, friend.

Robb Lentz, thanks for the way you pushed me out of my comfort zone time and time again. The ways you challenged and grew me developed the very skills I would need most as I stepped into this new calling. Thanks for showing me that I'm so much more capable than the false limitations I set for myself.

Ashlee Bell Wright, when I wasn't sure my words had any real purpose in this world, you showed up to show me otherwise. I needed that. PS: thanks for supplying the caffeine to get this thing finished.

A.D.—you know who you are, and you know why I'm forever grateful. This book would never have been completed without what you did for us.

And last, but most definitely not least, a *huge* thank you to *Megan Majors, Jenna Sturzinger, Angela Watts*, and anyone else who watched the boys at some point during this crazy process. There's simply no way I could have managed without your help.

Notes

Chapter 1

1. Flannery O'Connor, "Some Aspects of the Grotesque in Southern Fiction," in Sally and Robert Fitzgerald, eds., *Mystery and Manners* (New York: Farrar, Straus and Giroux, 1970), 48.

Chapter 2

1. William Goldman, *The Princess Bride* (New York: Ballantine, 2000), 141.

2. Andrew Wommack, "God Wants You Well," February 7, 2008, http://www.awmi.net/audio/audio-teachings/#/awm_1036a_atonement.mp3.

3. Gregory Boyle, "Father Greg Boyle," Facebook video, 7:10, from an episode of *I Love You, America with Sarah Silverman*, Hulu, November 9, 2017, http://www.facebook.com/ILYAmerica/videos/sarah-interviews-father-gregory-boyle/1885862141743066/.

4. "G2749—keimai—Strong's Greek Lexicon (ESV)," *Blue Letter Bible*, accessed January 9, 2019, http://www.blueletterbible.org/lang/lexicon/lexicon.cfm?Strongs=G2749&t=ESV.

Chapter 3

1. C.S. Lewis, *Mere Christianity* (New York: HarperCollins, 2001), 135.

Chapter 4

1. Alphonse de Lamartine, quoted in *Many Thoughts of Many Minds: Being a Treasury of Reference Consisting of Selections from the Writings of the Most Celebrated Authors*, comp. Henry Southgate (London: Griffin, Bohn, and Company, 1862), 265.

2. El Shama is not one of the names of God found in the Old Testament, but rather a Hebrew transliteration for the phrase "the God who hears."

Chapter 5

1. Brené Brown, Twitter post, May 3, 2017, 1:55 p.m., http://twitter.com/BreneBrown/status/859874176890490883.

2. "G627—apologia—Strong's Greek Lexicon (ESV)," *Blue Letter Bible*, accessed January 15, 2019, http://www.blueletterbible.org/lang/lexicon/lexicon.cfm?t=ESV&strongs=g627.

3. *The New Strong's Expanded Exhaustive Concordance of the Bible*, comp. James Strong (Nashville: Thomas Nelson, 2001).

4. "G1730—endeigma—Strong's Greek Lexicon (ESV)," *Blue Letter Bible*, accessed January 15, 2019, http://www.blueletterbible.org/lang/lexicon/lexicon.cfm?t=ESV&strongs=g1730.

5. "G5039—tekmērion—Strong's Greek Lexicon (ESV)," *Blue Letter Bible*, accessed January 15, 2019, http://www.blueletterbible.org/lang/lexicon/lexicon.cfm?t=ESV&strongs=g5039&ss=1.

6. "The Global Message of James," Crossway, accessed January 15, 2019, http://www.esv.org/resources/esv-global-study-bible/global-message-of-james/.

7. Robert F. Chaffin Jr., "The Theme of Wisdom in the Epistle of James," *Ashland Theological Journal* 29 (1997): 23.

Chapter 6

1. Timothy Keller, *Walking with God Through Pain and Suffering* (New York: Penguin Random House, 2013), 6.

2. Stephanie Tait, "I've Been in Pain," *The Joy Parade*, January 11, 2016, http://thejoyparadeblog.com/ive-been-in-pain/.

3. "G714—arkeō—Strong's Greek Lexicon (ESV)," *Blue Letter Bible*, accessed January 16, 2019, http://www.blueletterbible.org/lang/lexicon/lexicon.cfm?Strongs=G714&t=ESV.

4. "G842—autarkēs—Strong's Greek Lexicon (ESV)," *Blue Letter Bible*, accessed January 16, 2019, http://www.blueletterbible.org/lang/lexicon/lexicon.cfm?Strongs=G842&t=ESV.

5. "G2095—eu—Strong's Greek Lexicon (ESV)," *Blue Letter Bible*, accessed January 16, 2019, http://www.blueletterbible.org/lang/lexicon/lexicon.cfm?strongs=G2095&t=ESV.

6. "G1380—dokeō—Strong's Greek Lexicon (ESV)," *Blue Letter Bible*, accessed January 16, 2019, http://www.blueletterbible.org/lang/lexicon/lexicon.cfm?strongs=G1380&t=ESV.

7. "G2106—eudokeō—Strong's Greek Lexicon (ESV)," *Blue Letter Bible*, accessed January 16, 2019, http://www.blueletterbible.org/lang/lexicon/lexicon.cfm?t=ESV&strongs=g2106.

8. "Philippians 4:13," Bible Hub, accessed January 16, 2019, http://biblehub.com/interlinear/philippians/4-13.htm.

Chapter 7

1. Ann Voskamp, *The Broken Way* (Grand Rapids, MI: Zondervan, 2016), 221.

2. Information about shiva can be found at https://www.shiva.com/learning-center or through a local rabbi.

3. Rob Reimer, *Soul Care* (Franklin, TN: Carpenter's Son Publishing, 2016), 52.

Chapter 8

1. Craig Groeschel, Twitter post, September 3, 2013, 8:34 a.m., http://twitter.com/craiggroeschel/status/374918426327650304.

2. James Cone, *The Cross and the Lynching Tree* (Maryknoll, NY: Orbis, 2011), 156.

3. Walter Brueggemann, "Walter Brueggemann Q&A," YouTube video, 4:19, from a lecture at Wayne Presbyterian Church on October 18, 2013, posted by Casey Thompson, October 31, 2013, http://www.youtube.com/watch?v=0_YK0jTtj34.

Chapter 9

1. Barack Obama, "Barack Obama: Iowa Caucus Victory Speech," YouTube video, 13:13, January 3, 2008, posted by "BarackObamadotcom," January 4, 2008, http://www.youtube.com/watch?v=XB-sNaaaJRU.

2. K.J. Ramsey, Twitter post, August 27, 2018, 3:50 p.m., http://twitter.com/KatieJoRamsey/status/1034211506190086144.

About the Author

For Stephanie Tait, sorrow has never been the opposite of joy. Pain is the connecting point of grace and struggle that defines her career. As an author, speaker, disability advocate, and trauma survivor, Stephanie aims to do what she believes is sorely lacking in our trending conversations around Christianity—to partner sound theology and practice with the unashamed acceptance of struggle in the present tense. She aims to create space for the reality of sorrow, as well as offer practical tools and experience for its management, in the center of our faith ethic, our communities, and our joy.

From her home in Salem, Oregon—where she lives with her husband, Bobby, and two sons, Aidan and Jack—Stephanie has harnessed her experience, writing her intimate understanding of pain into messages that foster healing within the kingdom of God. Her commitment to equity, justice, honesty, and the theology of suffering makes hers a vitally refreshing viewpoint in an industry often overrun with relentlessly positive affirmations. One can serve God and struggle, celebrate and ache simultaneously, and it's Stephanie's hope that her stories and observations will grant others permission to arrive in their lives exactly and fully as they are. We all are dancing daily with the reality of sorrow, but together with grace, we can surround our sorrow with joy.

Website: www.stephanietaitwrites.com
Facebook: /stephanietait
Twitter: @stephtaitwrites
Instagram /stephanietaitwrites